M000232592

Amphibian Diaries

Amphibian Diaries

A Field Guide for Truth-Seekers

John Hansel, Jr.

ELM HILL

A Division of
HarperCollins Christian Publishing

www.elmhillbooks.com

Amphibian Diaries
A Field Guide for Truth-Seekers

Published in Nashville, Tennessee, by Elm Hill, an imprint of Thomas Nelson. Elm Hill and Thomas Nelson are registered trademarks of HarperCollins Christian Publishing, Inc.

Elm Hill titles may be purchased in bulk for educational, business, fund-raising, or sales promotional use. For information, please e-mail SpecialMarkets@ThomasNelson.com.

Cover design, images, and photographs by John Hansel, Jr.

Library of Congress Cataloging-in-Publication Data

Library of Congress Control Number: 2018957298

ISBN 978-1-595559654 (Paperback)
ISBN 978-1-595559661 (Hardbound)
ISBN 978-1-595559623 (eBook)

DEDICATED TO...

"My dear wife and fellow truth–seeker, Susie!"
(She kissed me, and I became her grateful prince.)

CONTENTS

The Heart for Home

Our heart is hungry for Love that's sure;
Our mind is thirsty for Life that's pure;
For deep within this bottomless soul,
We seek the Deep that makes us whole.
So life is spent as we live on earth,
Refusing to gain Love's lasting worth,
Till seeds of Truth to soul are sewn,
When Life grows New and heads for Home.
Each heart is restless till resting There,
Till souls confess to address this care,
So run child, chase what soul would own;
Run child run, with Heart for Home.

The Bayou

Darkness flowed like lava in the bayou, and the strangest sounds rose out of it. Swamp and shadows passed through each other. Black shapes stretched and seeped in every sliver of light as night crept into singular, sinister thickness. It was heavy and humid, laying over us. Still, everything moved in the sounds that encircled us.

Twenty years old and 1,000 miles south of home, I tracked a sense of adventure that made no room for sense in my head. I grinned my cocky, Cheshire cat best through the sweat beading over my lip. And I did my Yankee-Doodle damnedest to bury any fear beneath the most confident exterior I could muster, so far south of the Mason-Dixon Line. Then I heard it again.

It was closer—a low, grumbling clatter as if rising from deep within a dark, cavernous throat. It lasted five, no more than eight seconds, then ended with a clap, sounding like rocks snapping together. I heard it the first time just after we shoved off shore, when in the same moment I considered this place my two new friends brought me. My mind flashed to a scene from Jack Hanna's *Animal Adventures*— the head of a Holstein buried in the jaws of a Louisiana gator.

I wondered if Wayne Waggenspack or his buddy Roy Robechure had ever wrestled one. I asked, but I couldn't understand their answer. They were Cajun. They spoke a deep, Southern something, ladled through a heavy French accent. Every time one spoke, the other laughed, which reminded me of pigs squealing. So I got quiet, imagining pigs as the favorite food of gators.

Wayne steered our duck boat through the liquid black, the cold metal making a wake of steam through water that seemed to boil. Roy sat in the flat of the bow. I was in the middle, on the floor, where I could feel something tapping the other side of the aluminum hull. Roy whispered something, Wayne oinked, the boat shook, and I heard it again. In spite of myself, my head jerked in its direction—a muffled growl this time.

"Tat'l be da frowg," Wayne whispered.

Roy coughed a wicked laugh that echoed under the mangrove canopy. We ducked beneath the branches while Roy dug his knees into the bow and extended his belly over the water. He held an oar, high over his head, and whispered, "Na ya sees why we's ware'n dees heed-lats."

I followed the beam of his headlight with my own until both locked on a pair of green eyes shining back at us from the shoreline. Wayne explained this earlier as we drove to the swamp.

When a light is shined into the eyes of a frog, it acts like a frog-freeze ray. As long as the light is held to their eyes, they won't move. The frog becomes *a deer in the headlights*, stiff and stuck like prey on the end of an alien tractor beam, a prisoner of the force that wields the power of the light. Wayne and Roy had redesigned the hardhats we were wearing—a heavy flashlight welded to the top, connected to a sixteen-volt battery strapped to the back, with a reinforced chin harness for holding it to your head.

Need I say that Wayne Waggenspack and Roy Robechure

were seasoned frog giggers? That night—the only night I ever spent with them—I was their eager student, a rookie on his first ever *amphibious, amphibian safari*. Roy was locked and loaded. Wayne rolled his paddle in the water behind us until the boat fell into the line of the beam, then made one deep, sweeping stroke as a final push toward Roy's panicked but paralyzed prey. At that point, Roy's wide body blocked the view ahead. I imagined the glowing green eyes growing in our approach, which we made at a duck-boat version of *ramming speed*. I wondered if gator eyes glowed green in the light, too.

WHACK! Then *WHUMP!* Roy slammed the shore with his paddle in front of the flat of the bow, and he lunged in the direction of his strike, or he was thrown there. The mud caught him and most of his cursing, but Roy caught nothing except the full weight of Wayne's squealing and scorn as the first of our frogs hopped safely into the swamp. I tried to complement the ferocity of his paddle swing. That was received as the condescending pity of a Yankee, giving Wayne cause for another round of roasting.

Two minutes later, Roy was hung farther off the bow with paddle higher overhead. Wayne maneuvered the boat in the direction of another set of glowing green eyes, and I braced for impact with the shore. There was another *whack* and *whump*, with more muddy cursing and merciless scorning, as a second frog hopped to safety.

But before Roy could reposition himself for a third run, Wayne made him switch places with me. "Ya schkoold da Yankee wid yer gigg'n expertise." Wayne was clearly condescending. "Giv'm hiz try, Roy!"

Roy was smiling his version of that Cheshire cat grin as we switched places in the boat. I got the feeling he was expecting to swap stories of failed attempts. That and a Yankee's honor for the Union incentivized my energies as I took my place in the bow. I hooked my heels under the front seat and pried my toes against the bottom of the boat to secure me. Then I leveraged my thighs against the front flat edge of the boat and laid my torso out over the water, holding the paddle with both hands, high above and behind me. There were a hundred pairs of those luminous emerald eyes flickering in the beam from my helmet as I swept the shore with the light. I chose a set and locked in on them. Wayne caught my signal and began to quietly paddle me in the direction of my line of sight.

For a single, fearful moment, I thought about my situation from another angle. I was in the middle of a swamp with complete strangers who gave the impression that they could sell swamp to strangers. They claimed we were going to feed on frogs that we'd yet to catch. Now I was like a huge, live hood mount hanging off the front of Wayne's duck boat. As my body dangled over that bayou, I felt like bait. I wondered how many other Yankees had posed as gator chum off the front of a boat by Waggenspack and Robechure. Then I saw him.

The frog.

His eyes were frozen in my head beam, and the shoreline was fast approaching. He was huge; his body was a full four to five inches, not counting his legs, which would have been twice that. I wondered if the wooden boat paddle would be enough, but there wasn't time to ask. It was time for the Yankee to swing, and I wasn't about to miss. I slammed down on him with everything I had. *WHACK!* went the wood, and *WHUMP!* went the hull. In that split second the frog flopped over on its back as we slammed into the shore.

I don't remember how I stayed in the boat because I was completely focused on finishing my frog's gig. Roy had warned me that many a resilient frog had taken a beating, only to quickly revive, hopping off to freedom. In the next split second, I lashed out with my left hand, took hold of his legs as tightly as possible, then raised that fat frog over my head. When I knew I had him, I rolled over and back into the boat to proudly show off my prize. The boys were already howling.

But I couldn't. Another sensation quickly came over me. There was *something* in my pants, crawling up my right leg.

Instinctively I kicked and shook, trying to get it out, which the boys must have thought was some sort of crazy Yankee victory dance 'cause they whooped and hollered like I'd just scored a touchdown. But my little dance only caused whatever it was to crawl even higher inside my thigh and above my knee. I started to fear where this was headed. So with left hand still tightly wrapped around my frog flapp'n over my head, I unbuckled my belt and unzipped my pants with my right. Then I reached down and grabbed hold of the legs of what turned out to be...*another frog!*

I hoisted up my right hand to my left so that two frogs flapped over my head. Waggenspack and Robechure went silent with wonder for one brief second as they tilted their headlamps to my hands and let their eyes adjust to what I was holding. When those boys saw those two frogs, they lit into an explosion of hilarity that nearly upended us. Wayne kept slapping Roy on the back with one hand and the side of the boat with the other, as Roy repeatedly kicked at the bottom while wrapping his belly in his arms. Both were heaving in laughter, trying to catch their breath. I was sure someone might throw an aneurism.

Wayne, tears squeezing through his eyes, pulled at Roy's shoulder to turn his attention so they were face-to-face, and squealed, "Roy, ya'll was oh fer two…" He could hardly get the words out, but managed to add, "The Yankee was two fer one un he's first try!"

With that, all of us slipped from our seats and bounced heavily on the boat bottom as the cacophony of holler'n hilarity went to a whole new level.

It was some time and effort to gather ourselves before we could do any more frog gigging. But gigging we did. After I had my time hanging off the front of the boat, hauling in frog after frog, Roy finally got back into the swing. Then he and Wayne switched manning the helm so Wayne could have his way with a bunch of those poor frogs. An hour or so later, our sack was lumped full of Louisiana's finest frog legs, not a leg shorter than six inches, and some as long as ten.

When we made it back to Wayne's place, his father had the fryer stoked and ready for cooking. They call them "Louisiana swamp chicken," and for good reason. By the time the evening was over, our bellies were full of what tasted like the finest Chicken wings a northerner could imagine. Plus our sides split several times over for the story Wayne couldn't help but repeat about my two-fer-one frog gig, each time more embellished, especially for the size of the monster frog that came out of my pants!

It was all I could do to contain my pride for the thought of a Yankee becoming a part of what would undoubtedly be one more story in Waggenspack and Robechure's repertory of Louisiana lore.

Northbound

Thought of those frogs still had me laughing the next day as I boarded the plane to head home, north of the Mason-Dixon. Wayne and Roy kept me up much too late for such an early flight. So I was glad to see that only a handful of passengers joined me for the two-hour direct flight.

I found a seat as far from the others as possible, and told the attendants I would be sleeping so they wouldn't need to bother me for drinks or snacks. After takeoff, as soon as the captain announced we had reached cruising altitude, I flipped up the armrests and sprawled across three seats. I used my carry-on knapsack for a pillow. Another five minutes and I was R.E.M. 5, drooling and dreaming of a strange little man inside my pillow. I snored so loud, I woke myself.

I thought about what I'd just been dreaming: *A man in my pillow, how odd!* Yet I could still hear him. Either I was sleeping and dreaming, or a voice *was* coming from *inside* my knapsack. It seemed that laying my head there was causing someone quite a bit of discomfort because the voice was complaining from *within it*. And the moment I picked up my head, the voice was quick to thank me.

Slowly I sat up. And gradually I opened my sack to examine its contents. To my surprise, I found a frog. To my superlative surprise, the frog spoke. As clearly and as surely as one person speaks to another, the frog said, "How do you do?" Those were the first words he spoke to me, as pleasant and polite as can be—*How do you do?*—as if it were every day I might come across so friendly a fellow as a frog.

And just like the habit of such a courteous greeting, in spite of myself, I followed in kind. "Fine, I suppose," I said. "How are you?"

As I recall he said something about the weight of an average human head being ten pounds, which he estimated to be half a ton by comparison if it were laid on me.

"I'm sorry!" I heard myself say, and I knew I wasn't dreaming. But I had no idea what I was doing, because it seemed I was talking to a frog. And that wouldn't be so strange, if the frog hadn't talked to me first.

"A *talking frog*!?" that's what I said next.

"You're very observant," he said condescendingly.

Still put back, and now feeling somehow insulted, I responded as if it should be as obvious to him as it was to me. "Well, it is a bit strange, isn't it—a *talking frog*!?"

Then he started into the most rational line of reasoning. From that point on, he was always logically consistent. "Frog-talking is only strange when you first hear it. Have you forgotten how strange it was the first time you heard human-talking?"

I thought about children, what a difficult time they have talking at the start, and how a mother or father works to get that first syllable out of them: "Ma ma ma," "Da da da." *Yes*, as I thought about it, *what had become second nature to me, must have been very strange at the start.* But then I caught myself. "You are a frog talking as a human, *that's what's strange!*"

The frog continued. "Where I come from, frog-talking is as common as the banter of Waggenspack and Robechure. It is more intelligible, *and even more intelligent*, especially when you consider how a frog would never think to make sport of *man gigging!* Perhaps if you knew the names of each of those frogs as I do, beating them with paddles wouldn't come so easily. If you gave them a moment to express a word or two, in the next moment do you think you could throw them in the fryer?"

For a brief second, I thought about the gutting and cutting and frying of the night before, then attempted to redirect the undercurrent of sentiment. "Frogs have names?" It hadn't occurred to me until the frog introduced the idea.

"Each of us is different, much as the subtleties that distinguish your friends and you. Why shouldn't frogs afford each other the respect of the identity that comes with a name?"

His words and meaning still seemed to be headed for a boiling point. Then I remembered what I heard about frogs, water pots, and boiling points. So I attempted to reset the dialogue. "Hey, I feel like our conversation is set to *slow boil*, perhaps we could find something else to talk about while I get accustomed to a frog talking to a human."

"Very clever, young man, but I think in time you will find that it is *you*—your *self*—who needs to be saved from his slow boil, not me! In fact, that is the very reason you find me here in your knapsack."

I should have known. It's not every day a guy finds a frog in his bag, especially one that talks. It should have occurred to me that *the frog had a reason for being there*. But to save me? I had no idea what he meant. I could think of nothing from which I needed saving. Yet he was a *frog*. And he was *talking* to me.

Soul

I know my story is moving along before most are ready to believe me. It takes time for the mind to adjust to the thought of something so absurd as a talking frog. By this point in my account, most of you have already made a decision regarding the value of continuing. If you're still reading, then you're the kind of soul who is committed to doing so while suspending your judgments, at least to the point when I've made my point for telling the story. And if I'm willing to take the risk of being judged a nutcase for telling it, maybe you'll risk the chance to keep reading until you realize the value of the sense my new friend was making, regardless of his size, weight, and color.

— — —

"So you have a reason for being in my bag?" I asked.

"Of course I have a reason, and it was the same that sent me into that boat and up your pant leg last night. And if you should consider what risks I've taken to find my way into your knapsack, you might decide that there is value to hearing me out. You might conclude that my reason is a very good one."

I thought about what he was saying. Then I thought about who was saying it. "Well, I'm already talking to a frog. And hard as it is to believe, I'm also hearing the frog talk to me. If it's possible that we're actually having a conversation, then I probably should understand why. But you need to know, this all seems crazy to me already, so why should I think your reason any less crazy?"

"Ah, yes," the frog agreed, "but wouldn't you be even crazier if you chose not to hear my reason?"

What could I say? He wasn't *just* a talking frog. He was a frog talking sense in a way that I couldn't deny hearing.

"Perhaps," he continued, "you would be less prone to feel crazy if we had a more proper introduction. I gathered from your 'sporting' friends last night that your name is *Yankee*?"

I figured the informality of a nickname might protect me from any obligations to which this conversation might be leading. "Sure, Mr. Frog, you may call me *Yankee*. Please forgive me for not asking sooner—surely you understand my surprise. And with whom do I have the pleasure of... *talking*?" I extended my index finger to him, hoping that the formality of a handshake might indicate my willingness to take our conversation to a higher level.

The frog responded in kind, vigorously shaking my finger with more strength than I expected. He tipped his head as he said it, "BP... *BP Frog*, at your service, Master Yankee!"

"Well, BP, I acknowledge the energy and ingenuity required for you to be here next to me. And since we seem to have the back of this plane to ourselves, why shouldn't I hear you out in the time that remains of my flight back home?"

"Yankee, if you want to hear me out even halfway to the finish of what I have to say, then it will require more than the time it takes to get you back to that place where you make your bed tonight. And if you get even half of what you hear from me, then you will think twice about calling that place *home*."

BP was beginning to press beyond intrigue. His words induced a disquieting anxiety. I thought about it as the captain interrupted our conversation to announce that we were halfway to our destination, a place I had always referred to as home. "BP, I think it's time you get to your point." I worked up a timid smile and waited for him to begin.

He paused only a moment to adjust so that he was looking me directly in the eye. Clearly he wanted to make sure he had my attention. "My point," he said, "is *Life!*"

Anxiousness went to the next level. I thought about my strange situation. I was talking to a frog, 30,000 feet over sea level, traveling at the speed of a jet airliner. The night before I had been guilty of whacking and bagging and hacking and consuming a number of his kind. I thought about the only story I knew of a talking frog, enchanted by the curse of a dark witch. For a passing moment, I wondered if all of this would conjure word of some dark omen. I decided to confront my fear with candor. "I must ask, BP, are you the bearer of some sort of bad news? Is talking with you akin to a death wish? Is the plane about to go down?"

The frog laughed. It wasn't an incendiary or patronizing laugh but an adoring one, the kind a parent might make when his child expresses an honest misunderstanding. So I was relieved and believed him when BP assured me that he was a harbinger of *good news*. Then he added soberly, "But I must say with all earnestness, dear Yankee, each of us should fear one thing far more than death…that is, *never to have lived…*"

He repeated that last phrase, stretching it out through squinted eyes, and stilted with raspy whisper for emphasis, "*…Ne-ver—to—have—liiiiived!*"

All of a sudden I felt like Luke Skywalker with my own version of a little green Yoda.

"I'm not afraid," insisted Skywalker.

"You will be," warned Yoda. "Youuuu—wiiiiill—beeee!"

BP was tapping into a growing frustration I was already experiencing at a semiconscious level. My twenty-first birthday was a week away. I knew the date would mark an unspoken rite of passage that presumed me an adult. An *adult.* It sounded like something much farther downstream of the river of life. Certainly by now I thought I would have a better handle on the subject. But I felt like I was swimming upstream in the postmodern intellect of my enlightened culture. I was told that *life would be what I made of it.* I was trying to *embrace the emerging reality of what I wanted of life.* I felt that I could and should do anything, which somehow felt the same as nothing. If anyone wanted to live his life, it was me—*to the max.* But for what purpose?

The thought of a *meaningful* life was caught in an eddy behind a big rock, with a dangerous undertow, swirling through the rapids of life's river. As long as I could keep my head above the water, I was able to maintain a confident smile. But underneath I felt as though I was being pulled nowhere, much faster than I wanted to go.

BP smiled. "How can someone go…nowhere? On the

contrary, it is your recent admission of loss that turned your thoughts in this direction. Or have you not considered the connection between the truth of *Life* and the love of *Truth*? When a lost child decides to seek his Father, is it a coincidence to find the Father has long been seeking him?"

I laughed. I had no idea what he was talking about.

He patiently continued, waiting for me to make an important connection. "You have taken a long, hard look in the mirror, seeing all the way to your soul, but you've never come to the bottom of it. Rather you found yourself wanting for a life that is beyond you to live."

Immediately my mind went back to the morning of the day I boarded the plane on the front end of my trip to Louisiana. The eyes of my reflection were bloodshot, my head in a vice, my ears ringing as if I'd been dropped from a very high place the previous night. I couldn't remember if I'd had a good time. I had no idea how I was standing in front of that mirror. In fact, I wasn't sure who I was looking at.

"Where are you going?" That's what I asked the guy in the mirror.

A light went on, and I looked at BP who was sitting there in the seat beside me with a knowing look on his face. He extended his webbed feet and pulled himself closer to me. The whole time his eyes were locked on mine. He smiled ever so slightly, and I remembered the rest of the conversation with the reflection of my sad self that day.

"Where are you going!?" I asked again, surprised by my own frustration. I waited for an answer, and examined the blank look in my own eyes, like two openings to the hole in my soul, dark and bottomless. So I wasn't surprised when I answered my self. "I'm lost." I said it. I knew it was true. "I'm lost!" I said louder, expecting someone to hear, someone to care.

I remembered feeling disappointment. Not a whiney, "awe shucks" kind of disappointment, like when I was a kid and I didn't get the action figure I most wanted under the Christmas tree. This was much deeper; like after a lifetime of Christmas mornings, unwrapping present after present, expecting something new and different inside each box…something that could keep my attention and make me happy—keep me happy. I didn't even know for what I was looking. I just knew it had been a long string of disappointing surprises, so that lately I knew I would be more surprised to unwrap something of this world that could satisfy me.

Call me disenchanted, or disillusioned. I was disappointed at an existential level. The thought of it made me sink as I sat in the seat next to BP. It was the feeling of having lost something, yet I had no idea what it was. Still, looking, I couldn't find it. And unable to find it, I found myself…lost.

Truth Principle
The Soul with a hole.
We are all seeking a satisfying life.

"And lost, you are!" BP said to me as if he was able to hear my thoughts. "Yet, what human isn't? It is the nature of your species. For all of your civilized advancement, what new-fangled answer of humankind can fill the human soul, and set life free to the *Love* each heart is seeking? It is *beyond you.* The closest thing you have to the truth of *Love* is the truth that you don't have it. Hold on to that truth, dear Yankee. Seek by it. For that is your only hope of finding the freedom you desire. *Ask and you will be answered. Seek and you will find. In losing your life, you have a chance to find it!*"

EXPECTATION

"All right, BP, let's talk about life," I said to the frog, adding, "though, I must say, I wasn't expecting so heavy a subject from such a small fellow."

"I'll overlook that low blow," said BP, "because I think you'll find your ideas of life are too small for such a big-headed fellow."

"Okay, Frog." I learned early that I couldn't play a pun without BP jumping on it. "Let's get after it, because I'm hoping something good will come of our conversation about life."

"Ah, yes. That's just it, isn't it, Yankee? That is what everyone wants to come of life. Ask anyone…ask everyone on the globe what quality of life they want. Ultimately, won't they all answer the same? Doesn't everyone want a *good life?*"

Truth Principle
The **E**xpectation of Good.
We can only be satisfied by The Good Life.

"I suppose I wouldn't argue with that."

"Why would you?"

"Well, I might argue with your idea of what a good life is."

"But that's not my point here." BP illustrated, "Suppose I could ask everyone in the world a simple question, understanding that it can only be answered by 'yes' or 'no.'

Asking them, 'Do you want a good life?' Which way would you expect them to respond?"

It was a no-brainer. "All of us would say, 'Yes, I want a good life.'"

"So then," BP asked, "a good life is a universal desire of all humankind?"

"Yes. That seems obvious."

"Well then," he continued, "let's ask everyone in the world one more question. This time, the answer is open-ended: 'What is the good life you want?' How do you think people would respond?"

I said, "I suppose it is possible that all of us might have a different answer. Some of our answers might be similar, even the same. But many of our answers could be quite different, even polarized opposites."

"Yes, I agree," said the frog. "In fact, if you think about it, you humans find yourself in a dilemma with a magnitude of the first order when it comes to this first issue of your existence: *The search for the good life.* Each and every one of you wants it, yet not one of you can be sure what it is."

BP was scratching my itch. "Okay," I responded, "I think I follow where you're going. But so what?"

"So what!?" His eyes bulged. "*So what* is that every-body is living a life they want to be good, while at the same time they don't *know* what a good life is! It is the same as saying your existence is living for something of which you can't be sure."

"You said you had good news for me, Mr. Frog. This doesn't sound like *good news*."

"Yankee," the frog paused for emphasis, then said it

slowly so I wouldn't forget, "your thirst won't be quenched if you don't know you're thirsty! And great news is not good enough until you understand the bad news at its worst."

BP had a point and he wouldn't give up making it until it was fully understood. "Think of it this way: Each and every one of you humans spends your life worrying about and working at getting the good life you desire. Right?"

"Right."

"Well," he continued, "you worry about and work at getting the good life you desire while there is no promise you will get it, whatever you think *it* is! And if you do happen to get the good life you desire, then you will spend your life worrying about and working at keeping it. Right?"

"Yes. That's true also," I agreed.

"Then here's the thing. You worry and work to get something you've no promise of getting, and if you get it, you worry and work to keep it, while I can promise you this: *you will most certainly lose it.*"

That last statement caused me pause. In short time, BP found a way to stick his little frog finger in my open wound. My college graduation was less than a month away. Every time I thought about it, I would say to myself, *Graduate to what?* The question was looming over me as if my life should soon be set to some meaningful course. *You've one life to live, so make it count*, my father had said at least a thousand times. But count for what?

Then recently I was assigned a segment of Shakespeare's "Macbeth" to memorize for a class. It had a fancy name: *The Philosophical Rhetoric of Global Westernization.* It seemed an appropriate rhyme to the rhythm and meter of the frog's sorry subject. "Yes, yes, Mr. Frog. '*Tomorrow, and tomorrow, and tomorrow.*'" Somehow talking to a frog fitted the moment and me with a theatrical flair. "*Creeps in this petty pace from day to day until all our yesterdays have lighted fools their way to dusty death…*'"

To my surprise, BP the frog chimed in without missing a beat. "*Out, out brief candle. Life is but a walking shadow…that struts and frets its hour upon the stage, and then is heard no more…*"

We recited the last line together. "*It is a tale told by an idiot, full of sound and fury, signifying nothing!*"

The frog made a very dramatic bow, low, on bended knee and with a broad and high sweeping gesture of his right hand. It was the comedic relief I needed. I laughed. And BP smiled in spite of himself. But he wasn't about to let up on the seriousness of the point he intended to make.

"There's good reason the words of the bard have outlasted the test of time and human history, Yankee," the frog said. "The playwright stings with words that ring true in every lifetime. You and your upright, tall-standing, bipedal friends need to recognize the first two factors of your common existence…"

My new, little green friend had me just where he wanted. I was hanging off the edge of his last line, waiting for the next. He paused with one finger aside of his chin, as if he were carefully crafting his first few lines of a poetic wisdom that would run through the center of all he would say to me:

"Each of us is a *Soul with a Hole*,
So we run and run yet fall short of our goal;
We reset the bar *Expecting the Good*,
Yet never get far as we think we should!"

I know. It sounded mysterious, didn't it? That was the charisma of the frog. There were so many things he said that I didn't understand at the start. But he was full of truth so reasonably *and* tastefully spoken, that I couldn't help but want to hear more so I could eventually understand.

BP was as patient with me as I was forthright with him. When I told him that I didn't understand what he was saying or why, as in the case of his poem, he would repeat himself, rephrasing his words each time until he was sure that I was trekking with his meaning.

The frog wanted to impart wisdom to me. His message included certain factors for understanding life. They were principles of learning—*a code, if you will*—which he insisted would benefit me if I would be conscious of the factors and learn to apply them in life with others. As mentioned, however, the first two factors tended to set an uncomfortable tone at the start. But they were essential to understanding BP's overall message. Altogether, the message led to good news and the prospect of hope for living.

Before I recall any more of the story of my experience with BP Frog, I'll state his first two points of the code as clearly and concisely as possible.

FIRST: Each of us is a "**Soul with a Hole**." In other words, each of us possesses a natural desire for a satisfying life, which we are constantly seeking yet never fulfilling in this life. The search for satisfying life is at the center of our motives and actions.

SECOND: The satisfying life we are seeking is qualified, even valued, as something we sense we should have because we believe it would be good for us to have it. It is the "**Expectation of Good Life**," sometimes understood as an unalienable right. BP spent considerable time and effort explaining the frustrating implication of this factor. Namely, while we all somehow naturally expect a good life, we can't be sure what a good life is. And whatever we may think it is, there is no surety of getting it or keeping it, a truth that is inevitably exasperated by the brevity of our lives and our impending end.

Once I had a minimal and cursory understanding of these two points, BP knew I was ready to hear his next point.

ANSWERS

My new frog friend used his hands a lot. He made broad, sweeping gestures as he spoke, particularly when making statements of global implication as in his next point. "The most critical questions in all of life—*the Four Ultimate Questions*—are beyond each of us to answer," BP said. "The issues of our *Origin*, *Destiny*, *Meaning*, and *Morality* transcend our natural ability to comprehend with surety."

I think the frog sensed he shot that line way over my head, because he continued to press his message with four specific examples...

    (1) ***Origin:*** Where did we come from?
    (2) ***Destiny:*** What happens to us after we die?
    (3) ***Meaning:*** What is our purpose in life?
    (4) ***Morality:*** How should we live our lives?

"Surely there must be answers," BP continued, "yet we must make our way through this shadowy life, strutting and fretting without answers for questions we most certainly want to answer. Isn't this the very reason the bard called it a *shadow*? And come now, young man, we don't have long. Wasn't he also right to call it a *brief candle*?" He paused, and I knew he was waiting for my response.

I thought about a conversation I had with my grandfather who was waiting to die because he had fulfilled his final goal of reaching ninety years of age. Given the opportunity, he wanted to tell stories of his childhood. He would say things like, "*It seems like just yesterday*" and "*I can't believe how quickly the years have gone by.*" I decided to punt, "I'm not sure where you're going, BP."

His eyes bulged again. "You *miss* my point? You miss *the* point. You miss *our* point, *your point.* What you mean is, you're not sure where *you're* going!"

I realized then how much the frog sounded like my grandfather. I don't mean that his voice sounded old. I mean his voice was old, as in the way he spoke with wisdom beyond years, not *just* beyond frogs. So I said, trying to sound profound, "When you put it that way, Frog, does *anyone know* where they are going?"

He actually hopped when I said it, from the seat beside me to my shoulder. "That is my point!" he said with great emphasis. "How does anyone *know* where they are going? This is not something any one of us *knows* with *certainty.*"

He was pushing me to think on a grander scale, from a *global* perspective.

People sure seem to be going somewhere. Individually and collectively, everywhere and at all times, human beings are busy doing *something* for *some* reason. I turned to look out my window as the plane maneuvered a slight bank. There was a city sprawling out to the horizon beside us. I thought about the millions of people, now smaller than frogs or ants, more like microbes from this perspective. Each one, like me, was busily going about their business for one reason or another. Did they ask themselves *why*? Did they push for answers as deeply as the frog was now pushing? Do they expect sure answers and certain results? "Well, I will say this," I replied, "wherever they are going, they sure *think* they are going somewhere, and for *some* reason!"

BP cupped his little hands around his mouth, which was really rather large for such a small creature. He leaned from my shoulder into my ear and whispered, though I heard him very clearly. "No doubt, they are all very busily *going*, dear Yankee. But are they really *thinking* as they go? Are they *thinking* as we are *thinking* in this moment about our *going*? If they were *thinking*, could they be any more *certain* of what they say they *know*? Or, Yankee, my young friend, do we mean something different by what we are saying? What insight might we gain if we admitted that each of them plus you and I are going somewhere and doing something for what each of us *believes* to be *good reason*?"

I knew the frog was saying something important. He was scrutinizing the fabric of the truth of life itself, expressly as a messenger of some sort of *good news*. I wanted to understand him. "Mr. Frog, obviously, you are a unique creature and you have a particular reason for wanting to make a special message known to me. Please, speak plainly. Exactly what point are you trying to make?"

The frog hopped back to his place in the seat beside me. "I make no apologies for my methods, Yankee. For when it comes to *life*, it is critical that we *think*. We must *think about how* we *think*.[1] It is a competency that only *seems* difficult, especially when we are newly conscious of the reason, or ways, and means for doing so. Nonetheless, you are at the place where you are ready for me to make my point clear. Then you will be ready to move to the next point in my line

---

[1]   A developmental competency called, "Reflexive Thinking."

for our discussion of life. So I will speak it plainly. Just know that as I do so, as always, I proffer my claim as a truth of life, which is open to honest scrutiny born of continuing discussion. Do you understand this, Yankee?"

"I think so," I thought to say as I was thinking about my way of thinking while thinking about the frog's way of thinking. "You are about to make an important statement about life, which is part of the good news of life you are going to share with me. I think you are also telling me that what you are about to tell me is up for discussion in our ongoing dialogue about life."

BP smiled and said, "Thank you, Yankee. That was an excellent job of helping me feel as though you understand my meaning." No sooner had that complement come out of his mouth, and our plane dropped into a dedicated descent for landing, while the FASTEN SEAT BELTS light sprang to life on the console overhead.

"So," said the frog, "I will state my next point precisely, then leave it to you to ponder for further discussion, while you fasten your belt, and I make my way back to the safety of your knapsack." With his big bulging eyes, he fixed mine in his gaze, indicating it was time for me to closely listen. Then BP said, "When it comes to a discussion of life, everyone—and by that I mean *everyone*:

Everyone lives by faith!"

His eyes blinked once, slowly and definitively. Then BP crawled back into my pack.

A Wager

I don't know why I said it. It was the first thing that came to mind after the frog's big statement and as he was crawling into my knapsack. It was something my sociology teacher said to us one day during class. I repeated it then with the same proud tone the professor had used the day he said it. *"An atheist doesn't live by faith!"*

The bag moved. An eye popped out. Just an eye. Though what BP said was muffled, I heard him. "No one, not even the best atheist, can travel a single nanosecond back to before the big bang!" His eye widened, expecting me to get his drift.

I didn't.

He stuck his whole head out again and fixed both eyes on mine. It reminded me of the night before, lights in the eyes, just before the *whump* of the paddle to the head. But today was my gig. He spoke slowly to make sure I got his point. "If none of us existed before the big bang, then none of us, not even the most self-assured atheist, can say for certain—as if he were an eyewitness who might scientifi- cally record it—where we came from. On this we all live by faith. No one can claim some special advantage!"

I'd never thought of it that way before. As to atheists, they've always had an intimidating air about them, as if each of them thought they were the truest of scientist, basing all of their thinking upon the solidarity of material knowledge.

As if he could hear the conversation in my mind, BP reemerged from by bag, speaking loud enough I was sure the steward might hear him. "Let's get this clear, right from the start, young Yankee. Atheism is one more system of belief, and not the exception; a belief to which its adherents must work very hard to stick."

This was a new thought to me, and seemed sideways to my previous understanding, and I told him so. "I've never thought of atheism that way, Frog, and I doubt atheists do."

"Perhaps you hadn't…*thought*, human, and I wish our atheist friends would, also, *think* on this point." He ran into my bag for a second, then back out with a piece of my note-paper in his hands. He illustrated, "Imagine this page is a very special microcomputer. Yet it is the most powerful and amazing piece of paper, because on it, from top to bottom, resides all the information of everything in the universe."

I nodded my understanding.

"Tell me, Frog Gigger, how much of this paper would you claim to know? Take a pencil and make a circle that represents the portion of knowledge you have in relation to everything that can be known in the universe."

I pulled a pencil from its slot on the side of my bag and made a single, tentative dot on the page.

"I am surprised you made so large a mark, most intelligent Yankee," BP chided. "Now tell me…if 1,000 of the best and brightest atheist could be gathered, and their collective knowledge combined, make another circle to represent what portion of knowledge they would have in relation to everything that can be known in the universe."

I didn't want to make another dot next to mine. To BP's previous point, that would only inflate the estimation of my own *dot of knowledge*. So I made a tiny circle, intending to represent enough knowledge as 1,000 times my own, the size of a pinhead.

"One last question," promised BP. "If that dot and that circle represent all that you and 1,000 atheists could know of all that can be known of the universe, then how much is there that you all must admit you don't know?"

"A whole lot, obviously."

"And yet," BP pointed out, "an atheist sticks an 'A' on the front the word "theism" when choosing a label for themselves, why?"

I thought back to Etymology 101, and remembered the word "atheism" came from the ancient Greek language. So I responded, "The 'A' prefix is a way of negating the subject. So if by 'theism' one expresses the belief that *there is a God*, then they call themselves 'atheist' because they believe *there is no God*."

"Excellent, Yankee. And you have avoided my gig for now, because—whether you know it or not, you said it just as you should mean it. For given the limits to our knowledge of all things, that is the best an atheist can do—*believe* that there is no God."

I nodded. Then I prodded.

I was anxious to understand the full meaning of the frog's visit. "As you make your point, my new little frog friend, I realize you are making sense of life in a, theo*logical* kind of way." So I asked him, "By any chance, does the idea of *God* have something to do with you being here?"

A smile gently curled BP's lips and stretched his face, and his eyes widened into two large saucers, so that even from where he sat on the seat beside me it seemed he was looking down on me proudly. I don't mean that he looked proud. Quite the contrary, I mean he looked at me in a way that made me think he was very happy for me, like a mother for her child, or a teacher for his star pupil.

"There is great hope for you," he said. "You are intuitive to my direction, and there's direction because there's design."

I had no idea what he meant. Yet, somehow, I remembered what he said. With time, it took on great meaning. "It is a line on which you've landed," he continued, "the line was here long before you landed, and it extends far beyond the point that you could ever be right now. So the moment we start thinking in a way that could see some portion of that line with ourselves upon it, naturally the mind would come where the heart should want to go. For good reason, your reason is good."

I knew from that point on I would have to stay on my toes if I were going to keep up with the mind of that little frog. "Air traffic control to flying frog." Sometimes sarcasm was my only way of keeping the conversation in balance. "You've lost control of your altitude and you're flying way too close to the sun, Frog. Or you're way too high by means of some illegal stimulant. Either way, you're going to have to come down here for a minute to give me an idea of what you mean!"

BP laughed. "Ha, of course, you're right, new Yankee friend. I am too high. Forgive me. But I assure you, my stimulant is pure joy, and it is perfectly appropriate because your inclination is also right. The idea of God is the very reason I am here. In fact, *I am here to wager a bet with you!*"

The strangeness of my situation took on a whole new dimension. That the frog had made his way up my pant leg the night before and onto the plane today was strange enough. But this frog talked. And he was talking about God. As if all that wasn't strange enough, this frog was talking about *God* and *betting* in the same breath. "Now why shouldn't I be a bit suspicious? You want to make a bet with me? A bet about God? Gambling and God, isn't that a bit conflicting?"

"It depends on how you see it," the frog said, "because as far as gambles go, I think you will find that this one is impossible to avoid. It is the very nature of life. Insofar as each human lives by faith…it is the same as a wager. You bet your life—you bet *with* your life—each soul *spends life according to how they wager*." He leaned into me. "So how do you bet, dear Yankee? How will you spend your wager?" He paused for a moment as I considered his question.

Then BP continued. "I have heard many claim they 'have faith.' This is a strange way for people to speak of faith, for they mean it as if to say they 'have faith in faith.' Yankee, please be sensible and help pass the word, while hoping to open minds to reason. When a person says they have *faith in faith*, it is the same as saying they *bet on their bet*. Once you realize that each of us lives by faith, I hope you will see there is no escaping the reality of human existence:

> ***Each person lives life by faith as a bet***
> ***in the answers they believe to***
> ***the Four Ultimate Questions!"***

I said it again to myself, *Each person lives by faith—as their bet in the answers they believe—to the Four Ultimate Questions.* I thought about the many answers I had heard to the first question regarding Origin.

Of course there were many who believe that we are an effect of some cause that preceded us. I suppose most people on the planet believe we were made by some sort of God. And there are a growing number who believe we were seeds, planted by extraterrestrials. I also considered the idea of others, that we are *the effect of no cause.* For example, there are religions that believe we have always existed as a part of the universe. They believe we had no beginning—no origin—because we have always been "one with all things" as if we were one big, universal "god-ness." Then of course there were my atheist friends. According to most of them, if we had a beginning, it was an effect of no one personal, rather a random mix of certain elements, which eventually, by chance, formed in a meaningful way as the first of many random steps of the fittest to survive our evolution.

I wanted to test my thinking. So I asked the frog, "Even the atheist?"

"Yes, even the atheist. Each person has faith in some 'Thing' for the answers to those four critical questions. Tell me, Yankee, on what does the atheist place their wager?"

"I suppose *No Thing*," I answered.

BP pressed, "So the atheists believe in *no* answers to the questions of Origin, Destiny, Meaning, and Morality?"

I thought out loud, "That can't be. If a person doesn't have an answer to those questions, it doesn't mean there aren't answers. And if a person doesn't believe there is

Someone who can answer the questions, it doesn't mean there aren't answers. To *believe* there are no answers, or that there is no way to know the answers, *is a belief.* That's a bet!"

I convinced myself, and BP confirmed it. "And so, the atheist wagers their life, ultimately trusting their own idea, that there is no ultimate Someone to trust who would have answers to the ultimate questions that are beyond us to answer. You see, it's not a statement of value, but of fact… All of us, even the atheists, live by faith. We all wager, believing our answers to the ultimate questions. Therefore and thereby we live accordingly. It is the basis for our way of life."

That last sentence shot through my head and bounced around my mind like an echo in a canyon: *We all wager, believing our answers to the ultimate questions.* And I heard my heart reply, "What is *your* wager?"

The voice of the captain informed us that the plane was on its final approach for landing, and asked the attendants to fasten themselves into their seats. It was also BP's cue to reenter my knapsack, this time for good.

My heart replied again, *What is your wager?* But my mind had nothing to say. The silence was deafening and inescapable.

I was back in front of that mirror. And I said it again in spite of myself, "I'm lost!"

A Cream Puff

Once the plane landed, it didn't take long to get from my seat to the curb. With so few passengers, there was no line to disembark. I had only carry-on luggage, so there was no waiting in baggage claim. In short time, I was in the backseat of a yellow cab. But it seemed like the driver was taking a long time to find my apartment. Maybe it was my rush to get there. I wanted to get back to my conversation with BP.

The frog's last statement was bouncing around my brain: *"Everyone lives by faith,"* he said. The way BP said it, I knew it was critical to his reason for talking to me. Yet I knew the cab was no place to rejoin my conversation with a talking frog. Besides, I thought BP must be napping, because he didn't even venture to stick his head out of my knapsack.

A familiar song played on the cab driver's radio. For some reason he felt the need to push the volume. As he reached for the control, I noticed his nametag. It said, "TaxiZack." I wondered if he *lived by faith*, as BP said. I tried to imagine how TaxiZack might respond. As I did, I realized any answer he could have given to one of the four questions would prove BP right. Whatever his answer to Origin, Destiny, Meaning, or Morality, he would have to express it as a belief. I was beginning to think BP was right in his assumption about the universal faith factor of humans.

TaxiZack's song caught my ear and I tuned in. A guitar clicked away on the other side of the radio, tapping a steady, simple melody, sounding like a train gently ambling on its track. I could hear the guitarist's fingers sliding on the steel of his 12-string. I recognized the voice. It was John Mayer.

The words were haunting and drew me in. He sang of sleepless nights in light of a black-and-white reality of the unstoppable train of time through this life. I identified with him immediately. He wanted to get off the train and go back to the home of his youth, where *in his mind* everything was good and safe as it should be. He spoke of the fear of his parents dying and realization of life on his own. With open heart, the singer admitted his fear of getting older as the melody ticked away, his life flying by on the tracks. *Stop this train*, was his refrain. But in the end—alone in the dark—he admitted the truth we all must to come to: *No one can ever stop the train!*

I'd heard the song before. But never like I heard it in that moment. My eyes were wet, and I didn't want TaxiZack to know. But I looked up in spite of myself. Our eyes met in his rearview mirror. His eyes were wet, too. We noticed the *other*. Our souls touched for a brief moment; both of us knew it. We could feel each other hanging over a dark, bottomless place that yawned and yearned at the same time, searching for something we had yet to find.

I looked away. The light turned green. TaxiZack went back to his driving.

"Pullover up ahead, please!" I was startled. It was BP from inside my knapsack.

TaxiZach thought nothing of it, surely thinking it was me. He pulled over.

I knew the place well. It was the vacant lot at the corner

of Lane Avenue and Northwest Boulevard, a point equidistant between the home where I grew up and my current apartment. With the words of that song still fresh in my head, I realized it was also the symbolic point somewhere between my youth and growing up, *being out on my own*, as the song said.

At that corner every Monday, a food truck would park to vend for drive-by customers. It was *the sausage truck*. The family that owned it was known for generations of its famous brat, the "Brat-Mama-Bomba." But they're also credited with the best cream puffs on the planet.

One per week, that was my guilty pleasure, each and every week on the way home to my apartment from school or work. I would starve myself from dinner the night before, to make room for the calories—nearly 335 per puff. It was mostly custard pudding, heavy vanilla cream, eggs, and sugar, whipped smooth then smattered and smashed between two fluffy pastry buns. Andy, the truck manager, had become a good friend—the supplier of my habit for nearly three years. That's how long he had been setting aside the biggest, creamiest puff for his most faithful Monday-afternoon customer.

"Man," Andy spoke first, "you're an hour early. The cream puffs are still in the oven!" He was a big man, who seemed even bigger when he looked down at you from over the counter of his food truck.

What could I say? It wasn't my idea to be standing there and then. If not for Andy's disarming smile, I might have been self-conscious and fumbling for words. "Just stopped to say hi on the way to my apartment. The cab driver over there is waiting for me. Can't stay long." There were Mondays when Andy and I spent hours jawing about one thing or another. I had no idea what BP had in mind for this unscheduled stop. But I was the one who would have to pay TaxiZack, so I was intent on keeping it brief.

"It's almost like you had your antenna up, or your ears were burn'n," Andy chided. "Did you pick up some new telepathic ability while you were down South? How'd you know I had something special for you?"

"Oh, I picked up something, all right," I responded, "but it doesn't have antenna, so I have no idea what you're talking about."

I'd forgotten, I told Andy I would be traveling to Louisiana. It seemed he never forgot a thing, about anyone. Once, I asked him how and why he was so good at remembering stuff about people. His response surprised me. He said he *prayed for all his friends.* So I figured him as a person who believed in God. But I'd never thought of Andy as one of those *religious nuts* who preached their beliefs down your throat.

On the contrary, I'd known Andy as a regular guy who'd had me over to his house on more than one occasion for a ballgame and beers. He seemed genuinely happy, as if he possessed a firm handle on life. There was a peace about him, and a trustable, approachableness that I never experienced in many people. So what happened next didn't seem so strange or out of place. In fact, somehow I knew it had everything to do with BP's impromptu stop.

"I have an invite for you," Andy said. I figured it was for another game, or a party at his place as I took the postcard from his hand. In the other he extended a cream puff to me. "The cream puff is on the house 'cause I feel bad, having to give you one of the day-olds. But I told you, today's aren't ready yet. And the invite…well, take the week to think on it. Tell me how you feel about it next week when you stop by."

A nudge at my back from BP within the knapsack was sign enough for me to know we had what he wanted. I thanked Andy, apologized because I couldn't stay, and turned to walk back in TaxiZack's direction. By the time I reached the yellow door of the cab, I'd already read the front of the invite envelope.

An Invitation to…
The LIFE-Bet
Conversations about God and Life

As I reached for the door handle, BP called to me from over my shoulder and inside my bag. "Wait! Before you open that door…"

I froze, my fingers inches from the handle. I must have looked silly to TaxiZack.

"Before you open that door, and before you open that invitation, if you have any thought of taking up Andy on his invite, then you must exchange promises with me," BP said.

I knew in that moment there was a direct link between my strange experience with the talking frog and the invite that my friend just handed me. Even so, I wasn't about to end my conversation with BP anyway. I mean, think about it: How often did a guy get that kind of opportunity? I was a born storyteller. I lived every day for a new experience to share with others. And this one was adding up to one hell of a story. My only challenge would be how to tell it so that someone might believe me. Whatever BP was there to talk about, I wanted to hear. But up to that moment, all of the surprises that day had been thrown in one direction: mine. For whatever reason, I decided to turn the table for a moment, if for nothing else then just to see how my mysterious friend would respond.

"I'll think about it. " That's what I said, then I quickly opened the door.

"Wait!" BP was adamant, and this time loud enough that I was sure TaxiZack heard him. "We must exchange promises!"

As I slid into the backseat of the taxi, I didn't care anymore about TaxiZack listening in. "I said I'll think about it." I tried to respond with equal resolve.

The frog went silent.

"Think about what?" asked TaxiZack, sure I was speaking to him.

I decided the irony of my situation was too loud, too obvious for anyone to believe. "Oh, I wasn't talking to you. I was talking to my frog."

The driver laughed as the truth flew by him without another thought. "Shall I take you to your destination now?"

I nodded and we were off.

BP said nothing, he didn't even move. It was my move. From the side of my mouth and over my shoulder,

I whispered so only the frog could hear. "I said I'll think about it. I thought part of the reason you were here was to get me to think. Well, I'm thinking." For some reason, I was enjoying the moment, being cynical, a bit incendiary even.

Conflicted

It was a ten-minute drive from the corner where Andy and the cream puffs were parked to my apartment. It was time enough to think about the invite he'd given me. Curious circumstances were drawing me into something. The timing of the invitation and BP's visit flowed through a confluence of issues that I knew were rapidly moving my life forward. But *to what?* That question loomed as large as this messenger was small, and the contrast was a comical accent. I couldn't ignore what seemed to be intentional, and therefore important for me.

But I also felt cornered. My friend Andy had given me an invitation to *conversations about Life and God*? How would a guy turn that down without coming off closed, or shallow? Plus it seemed too intimate a subject to me, like talking about sex. Somewhere in my soul I had a sense of hesitation. There was fear beneath my cynicism. Stubbornly, I felt an urge to fight back, though I had no idea why, or against what. A poem I memorized in a ninth-grade English class popped to mind, and I wanted to scream, "*I am the captain of my soul!*"

> *Out of the night that covers me,*
> *Black as the pit from pole to pole,*
> *I thank whatever gods may be*
> *For my unconquerable soul…*[2]

---

[2] The first two stanzas of "Invictus" by William Ernest Henley

A minute later, TaxiZack pulled into the parking lot of my apartment complex. It was four stories of twenty flats, situated on the east shore of the bay with a full view of the western sky. Thanks to an athletic scholarship, I gladly paid a premium rent for my pad, which was intentionally built with an orientation to the most beautiful view of the bay. TaxiZack scanned the digs and immediately started angling for his tip, saying something about how *I must have a bunch of high-rollers for friends*. I paid him cash, telling him to keep the change.

"Thanks," he said. Then offered, "One tip for another?"

"Sure," I replied.

"Don't forget, the train can't stop, friend…so let's make the most of it!"

"I feel you, man." I chuckled. "Catch you next time."

"Hope so!" *That was the last thing he said.*

There was something in the way he said it that caused me to throw one more look in his direction as I closed the door. For a brief second, I thought I was looking at BP, as if his green face was superimposed on TaxiZack's. He reached forward and cranked the radio while he pressed the pedal. I could hear him rocking to Petty as he drove off. *"I won't back down,"* the words trailed as he rode away. I knew the defiant lyrics of the next line, and I heard them in my mind, something about *not backing down even at hell's gates.*

All of a sudden, a flood of songs rushed through my head as if coming from every direction, clashing in my mind, title by title. It was like the battle of the bands in my brain.

"I Can't Get No Satisfaction," admitted the Stones.

"But it's 'My Life,'" Billy Joel demanded.

To which the Arcade Fire replied, "'Lies'!"

"So 'Run On' if you can," warned Johnny Cash.

"But 'Don't Worry Be Happy,'" tapped Bobby McFerrin.

And I was deep in Dillan's "Subterranean Homesick Blues."

It left me wanting—no, needing some semblance of "The Good Life." (Rock on, Three Days Grace!)

The good life! BP! The cab had driven away! For a moment, it occurred to me that BP might have driven away with TaxiZack. I was filled with immediate regret, and sank. My last impression was BP's face on TaxiZack! Had my little friend left me?

My head started to spin, and I thought I was going to be sick. I turned to head in the direction of my apartment. As I did, I couldn't help but notice the blue of that wide-open, late-afternoon sky over the bay. The light of the sun was hitting the waves at just the right angle, so that I had to shade my eyes from the sea of shimmering sparkles as far as I could see. The breeze was slight but constant, so that the sound of someone's wind chimes in the distance set the perfect sound track to a million ripples in the water. The bay was beautiful, again.

Why?

That's the word that spontaneously formed in my head. *What an innocuous, volatile, huge, little question*, I thought to myself. I remembered those four critical questions BP had introduced an hour earlier during the flight: *Origin, Destiny, Meaning*, and *Morality. We wager the answer with our lives. Why?*

I thought about the simplicity and gravity of that single question. It was like a black hole to my soul, captivating and cavernous at the same time. I found myself hoping there was hope. I wanted to explore the chance that there was, but *had I blown my chance?* I just stood there. I wanted to ask BP. But I was afraid to because I feared there would be no answer.

"Why?" I heard again, louder.

I realized the question was coming from inside my knapsack this time rather than from inside my head. "BP?" I said sheepishly. "Are you still here?"

"Of course... Why?" I heard the frog say, muffled through the bag.

I couldn't tell you how happy I was to know that BP was still with me. I'd only known him for a couple hours, but I'd become quite fond of him. Somehow I knew he was a friend, and though I had my doubts—even fears about the direction our conversation was headed—in the short time I knew him, BP had already convinced me that his intentions were for my best interest.

"Why are you struggling with such obvious questions?" I heard him ask. "Why wouldn't you want to talk about these things with such a good friend as Andy? Why? What is the harm in it? Why would you not exchange promises with me so you could hear the rest of my message to you? Please, why not take a seat on your favorite bench and tell me, dear Yankee? Surely this place will always be important to you. It is the perfect spot for us to talk."

My hair stood up. How could he have known about *the bench*? Did he know how often I sat there, nearly every evening, to watch the sun set on the other side of the bay?

Just then, I realized the last time I'd sat in my bench. It was just before my flight, south to Louisiana, a week earlier.

The sky was intoxicating, full of colors in the sunset that evening. I felt as though I could drink it, like a smooth peach schnapps. There had been a short summer rain burst, so there was a full rainbow that stretched from one end of the bay to the other. In the distance, every five seconds or so, flashes of lightning would fill one cloud after another that hung in a line across the horizon. The clouds seemed to be in conversation, and the rumble of their quiet chat rolled over the bay in the waves to my little bench.

I was alone.

It was as though the entire display was for me. And I felt the urge to thank someone for the show. *But who?* I asked myself. And then I heard my mind respond, *Why do I think I should thank someone? Why?* The answer seemed somehow obvious to my heart. Even so, that cynic repeated, *Why?* It was the same cynical voice that shut down BP in the cab.

Being alone I felt alone. So from someplace deep inside me, which must have been my soul, I said out loud, "Why?"

That night a week ago, I waited for an answer until the sun was buried in the lake and the colors had faded into the cool of the evening. The entire experience was forgotten in the darkness. I walked up the stairs to my apartment, gathered my things, called a cab, and was off to the airport to catch my flight South. Then upon return, in that moment, I realized I was sitting there again, this time with BP, the talking frog.

And here it was again, the question: *Why?* BP and I were picking up where I left it that night on the bench.

Benched

I took off my knapsack and laid it on the bench beside me. BP crawled out and sat there, looking at me looking at him. I wondered whose turn it was to speak. It was an uncomfortably quiet moment, except for a soft gust of wind chilled by its trip across the bay to our seat. It was a perfect complement to the heat of the sun, forming beads of sweat on my forehead. I decided to pick up where we left off. "So what's this business about promises we have to make to each other?"

BP parried my nonchalance to reset the moment to his pace and demeanor. "The wind blows wherever it pleases," he said. "You hear its sound, but you cannot tell where it comes from or where it is going."[3]

I said, "I suppose so," trying to hold on to a protective layer of indifference, not knowing what was coming.

"Coming and going. Origin and Destiny," BP responded. "Clearly we can't deny their place in our life. And surely we're foolish to deny the meaning of our place between them in time. Yankee is here. I am here. But there is a beginning and an end. Who marks these?"

I had nothing to say.

"Come on, Yankee," he prodded. "There is a track and a train, and it is trekking somewhere. Where is all this going? TaxiZack's song was enough to wet your eyes. Let it wet your heart and the appetite of your soul, as well. What do you know? Where does it go?"

Still having no response, I decided to reply in the frog's

---

[3]   John 3:8

words from earlier. "That's a matter of faith for us all, isn't it, frog?"

BP's reply was another surprise. "Of course you are right to say we all live by faith when it comes to knowing these things. But that doesn't mean there isn't an answer. Go ahead, Yankee friend, tell me there is no answer. Tell me all this comes to nothing. If I ask you what will come of you and your loved ones after you die, tell me nothing, because you will no longer exist."

"I'm not going to say that," I said, "because you'll just point out that I can't know that to be true. The pure materialist or naturalist who says 'this is all there is' lives by faith, the same as everyone else."

"Yes. I'm glad you see that is true. We are all the same, living by faith… But not all faiths are the same."

"Well, that seems obvious, but I think I ought to chew on it," I said.

"Good idea. Think about this: whatever the truth of reality is, when we finally come to it, reality will prove the value and veracity of, what was to that point, our faith…our belief about reality."

I didn't know what to say. What could I say? But BP knew I was thinking. He had me thinking about my thinking, again.

He continued. "The Source of all Life and Love put it in the heart of your friend to invite you into a conversation. And I am here to prepare you for it. Your friend presented you with that invitation right on schedule. But there are promises that you and I must exchange before you open and read it."

"Mr. Frog, I'm not sure how it is that a frog talks, or

how it is that I think I can hear a frog talking. But I think your reason for being here must be pretty important. When we stepped out of the taxi, there was a brief second when I thought I'd lost you, and my feeling of regret was instantaneous. I don't know how long you're going to be around, but as long as you are here, I want to hear what you have to say. So lay it on me," I replied. "What are the promises we have to exchange?"

"For your part, Yankee, you must promise that you will hear me out. Thus far, on this matter of the life of faith, I've only shared three of six claims with you: the **S**oul with a hole, the **E**xpectation of good, and the **A**nswers from outside the Box. Before you open that invite," he said, "I ask you to allow me to finish sharing with you the remaining three principles of the Search… **R**, **C**, and **H**."

I thought about the quality of the encounter with the frog to that point. I wish you could've been with me. I wish you could've met BP, heard him speak, seen him smile, sensed his positive intentions. It was disarming each time I thought about the peaceful presence he seemed to exude. Whatever he was going to say, I knew it would be the word of a friend. Whether of his own plans, or BP was mediating the ideas of someone else, strange as it was, I had the sense that he was no stranger. I knew his purpose was to affect the good of some intention with a view to my best interest.

Before BP said anything more, I decided I would promise to hear the frog through to the end of what he had to say before deciding about the invite, and I promised him so. Then I asked him, "What is the promise you will be making to me?"

"I have come to you in the spirit of friendship and I will hold Andy to the same. And," BP continued, "I promise to maintain that spirit throughout our time together. There are decisions to be made—large, important decisions. But they are yours to make. However you choose to proceed from this moment forward, as your friends, Andy and I must maintain a gentle and respectful posture, with your best interest in mind. That is my commitment, and I will do my best to hold Andy to the same."

Again, I still had no sense of what was coming. But the mystery surrounding BP's visit was full of intrigue. Plus my experience with the frog to that point had been delightful. Whatever he meant by a need for gentleness and respect, I decided I could trust him for it. "Sure, Frog. I promise to hear you out before I open the invite. And I accept your promise of friendship."

The frog smiled, very satisfied.

In that moment, there was another gust of wind, but powerful this time, and warm. I felt as though I'd been abruptly wakened from a dream, my attention drawn out across the water from our bench. The sky was big and blue in the late-afternoon sun, as far as my eyes could see out over the bay. And there in the middle of it was a single cloud formation. I tell you, as sure as I am writing this, the cloud formed a giant question mark, as if to punctuate the moment. I looked around, wondering if anyone else had noticed.

I sat there, jaw dropping. And BP, still smiling, said it all. "They are such important questions, aren't they? How could anyone ignore them? Why would anyone ignore them? Why?"

Please believe me, this is an actual picture of the cloud that day.
Something this special, this spectacular, can't be for me alone.
This is one more reason I had to write this book!

The Box

I ran up four flights of stairs, and I unlocked the door to my apartment. For a moment, I thought about how hungry I was. But the excitement of what I had just experienced had me wanting to get back to the discussion with BP. It was overriding my hunger, even though I had missed breakfast and it was already well past noon. I went straight to my bedroom and threw myself and my knapsack on the bed, thinking the mattress was soft enough to receive us both. The knapsack bounced with me, and I could hear the frog's displeasure inside.

That's when I noticed the white cloud of powder billowing from the sack. Only then did I remember that I put my body powder in it as I was packing that morning. And it wasn't until I opened the bag that I realized I hadn't secured its lid. The entire inside of the bag was covered with a layer of white dust, along with all of its contents.

That's right. My formerly little green friend hopped from my knapsack looking like the ghost version of his self. (I wouldn't dare tell him, but he looked like his friends from the night before, after we rolled them in flour, and before we threw them in the fryer.) For a second I thought he'd gone the way of his friends, and I'd heard the last from him. Then he coughed and poofed a little white cloud of powder. I made the mistake of laughing.

BP found no humor in the situation and told me as much. For a moment, each word he spoke was accompanied by a tiny powder poof. I couldn't contain myself and fell to the floor in uncontrollable laughter. If not for the patience and honor of the little green sage, I was sure I would have heard the last from him. A lesser frog would have found his way back to the bayou.

Within a few moments I was back to my senses. Containing my laughter, I gathered up BP and carried him to the bathroom. Then I gently placed the frog on the bottom of the porcelain tub basin, assuring him I'd get him cleaned up, while suggesting he might even enjoy the process.

My hunch was confirmed when I turned the water on. BP actually managed a white, powdery smile as the water began to swirl around him. Once it was deep enough, the frog pushed off and started swimming. By the time he'd finished his first lap around the tub, he was back to green. I shut off the spigot, and he sat on the basin bottom at the shallow end, his head above the water, and looked at me with those big eyes of his. When I noticed they were burned red by the talcum, I busted into another laugh. Thankfully, BP joined me this time, and said something about *being glad to give up that ghost.*

I apologized for testing my new friend's faith in me. BP jumped on my choice of words. "Funny you should put it that way," he said. "For the *test of faith* was the very subject we were about to discuss. Do you recall the statement I last made to you regarding faith?"

How could I forget when a talking frog made the point, especially when he made it so emphatically? "You said that *everyone lives by faith.* And you were careful to empha- size the word *everyone,* as if you were making a universal claim about life. Then your illustration regarding atheists was effective."

"Well, as important as remembering my claim, have you thought about it?" This would be a point the frog would make over and over out of a general concern he had for humanity. According to BP, we'd advanced by technology to a dangerous, backward place where phones were smart enough to keep us busy *through a day* while dumbing us down for the business of thinking *through our days.* "What do you *think* of the assertion that *everyone lives by faith?*" he asked again.

"When you use the word *faith,* it sounds like you are making some sort of religious statement," I responded. "If that is what you are implying, then I can't agree with you. There are a lot of people who are not religious and a bunch of science-minded folks who would tell you they don't live by faith. An agnostic person, for example. They don't live by faith; they live by fact."

"My statement is not religious," the frog said with a proud smile, "and the agnostic does live by faith. In fact, the *atheist* lives by faith, though both the agnostic and the atheist are not religious."

I scratched my head. BP understood my itch, so he continued. "By definition, agnostics say that they *don't know of God,* and the atheists say there is *no God.* So neither believes *in* God, and therefore they aren't religious. I wouldn't disagree with you on that point. But I wasn't making a point of religion. I was simply saying that everyone lives by faith, which is to say everyone believes something when it comes to the hole in the human soul and the expectation of a good life. Don't forget our *strutting and fretting* during *our hour upon the stage.* We're all stuck in the Box, including our agnostic and atheistic friends, and every form of naturalist and materialist with them."

BP had introduced a new idea at that point. I had to ask, "What's that you say, we're all stuck in *the Box*? This is the first I've heard you speak of *the Box*."

Truth Principle

Answers from Outside The Box.
We trust we will be satisfied by our answers.

He corrected, "Actually, we *have* spoken of it, but not yet as *the Box*. When I mentioned those four critical questions of life, we were speaking of it. The ultimate questions of our Origin, Destiny, Meaning, and Morality demonstrate that we are in *the Box*. Inside the Box, those questions can't be answered with *certain* knowledge."

I wanted desperately to demonstrate that I was thinking about the things BP was saying. "It seems that you are talking about space and time. We're all stuck in it. It's not as if any one of us can jump beyond the dimensions of our existence or break the bonds of time. No matter how many times I watch *Back to the Future*, Steven Spielberg and Michael J. Fox and I are still getting older as we strut and fret our hour upon the stage."

"Precisely," agreed the frog. "Now you're talking *the Box*. We can't precede our existence. Even a talking frog can't go back in time. Not even an agnostic or atheist can go back one nanosecond before the big bang. They can't *know* from experience where we came from or how we got here any better than anyone else. Whatever answer they give for that ultimate question of Origin, they are merely telling you what they *believe*."

I was on his wavelength. I tried to anticipate his next statement. "So the atheist and agnostic also can't precede *or succeed* our existence. In other words we can't go into the future and beyond our deaths to answer the question of Destiny, either."

"That's right," agreed the frog. "Religious or not, and no matter how scientific anybody may be about it, not a one of us has the natural ability to go into our future and beyond life, then to come back and tell us about their experience. In this sense, whatever we claim about these things and our ultimate Meaning and Morality, we make our claim based on what we *believe* about them, not what we *know*."

"It sounds like you are leveling the playing field when it comes to the Box," I noted.

"There you go. Go on, Yankee," he encouraged.

"Well it seems to me that there is constant bickering between people of science and people of religion as if one or the other is superior in its way of approaching these things. But in the end, Ms. Science and Mr. Religion are both limited to what they can know *in the Box*. When it comes to the ultimate questions of life, as you say, *everyone lives by faith*, in the way they answer. Maybe Shakespeare would have called this the *shadow* in the box of life, which has us sometimes *strutting* and other times *fretting* for what little *light* of *the candle* we may have for the subject inside the box."

"Now you're talking, Yankee." BP was hopping and splashing. "Yes, I think you are understanding my point exactly. The Box has a bottom line, so to speak. The critical questions of life have a ceiling, the top of the box, the top line, a limit beyond which no one may go for certain answers. Each of us is limited to their system of beliefs in answer to these questions, so that all of us—in this sense—*lives by faith*, by the way they go about answering the four questions. Sure answers are naturally beyond each and every one of us in time and space, here and now. So when you think about it, whoever you are, whether you are Ms. Science or Mr. Religion, as you say, *life is a bet*!"

BP decided I was ready for the next verse of his code that contained the thread to his line of reasoning. He recited it then and there from his spot in my tub…

Each of us lives as a ***Soul with a Hole***,
So we run and run yet fall short of our goal;
We reset the bar, ***Expecting the Good***,
Yet never get far as we think we should!

———

Our questions have *Answers* from outside the Box
So we live by a faith that guides our thoughts

The Code

"Ribbit."

That's what BP the frog said. But he didn't belch it like a frog croaking, so it wasn't the sound I heard, but rather the word, as if you or I were speaking it. He sat there in my tub on all fours, eyeballs, head and slimy shoulders above an inch of water in the basin, and spoke it again with a smile on his face this time. "Ribbit and *croak*," he said again, like a little green man.

"You know, I think I could croak better than that, Mr. Frog," I said to him

"I suppose you could, Yankee," said the frog, "for already you seem to be *thinking* as well as a frog." He smiled again.

BP Frog's humor was subtle but effective, affecting a backdoor compliment, which I appreciated. He used these obtuse nonverbals and humorous puns to carry me between the points of his line of reasoning, ensuring I stayed with him as he moved from one important statement to the next.

"This poem you're quoting," I interjected, "it seems to be central to what you want to say to me."

"You're very perceptive," he encouraged. "And I suppose you're ready to hear the rest of it, that is, if I may first spend just a moment to preface the poem so that my purpose is not lost in it."

Then, before reciting it, he reminded me that I had promised to do my best *to understand his meaning for each line of the poetic code.* Over time I had learned to appreciate the code as the first part of his unique message—a test of wisdom for intelligent interaction between thinking persons, and a means for *discussing and discovering* the essential truths of God and life together.

I don't know that I would have seen it if he hadn't shown me. The poem contains six essential elements to BP Frog's formula, which are spelled out for those who would genuinely *search* for the truth of our existence. The acronym—S.E.A.R.C.H.—is a helpful mnemonic for recalling the poem and the line of his reasoning running through it.

> Each of us lives as a ***Soul with a Hole***,
> So we run and run yet fall short of our goal;
> We reset the bar, ***Expecting the Good***,
> Yet never get far as we think we should!

———

> Our questions have ***Answers*** from outside the Box
> So we live by a faith that guides our thoughts
> That wisdom would try by test of ***Reason***
> In search of good that's right in each season

———

> So pry and try the ***Corresponding perception***,
> And examine each thought by trial of reflection
> *To search for the truth that's **Humble** and whole*
> *For purposeful life and peace for the soul.*

After reciting the poem, BP proceeded to enumerate the code of principles running through the lyrics, identified by the S.E.A.R.C.H. acrostic. "If you miss these," he warned, "you will miss the meaning of my verse, and worse yet, you risk missing altogether the reason for my visitation to you." He presented them as six principles, each of which is a key factor in the process of conscientious, competent learning for understanding life:

1. The **S**oul with a Hole
2. The **E**xpectation of Good
3. The **A**nswers from Outside the Box
4. The **R**eason we trust
5. The **C**orresponding Perception, and
6. The **H**umble Heart.

This was first time the significance of my conversations with BP Frog dawned on me. When he listed those keys, I realized my experience wasn't going to be one more fun story to tell friends from my crazy life of adventure. The frog had an important life message that he intended to pass on to me. He was expecting me to remember the principles he shared, as if they were critical to understanding life. I learned that he intended for me to repeat his lessons, to somehow recall and reclaim them in as broad a manner possible among the members of my species.

"Forgive me for being so slow about this, Mr. Frog," I apologized, "but as you recite the code and list these principles for me right now, I realize that you are a serious guy, and all of a sudden I think my sense of the fun of talking with a frog is not the game I thought it was. I feel like you are signing me up for something more intense than I surmised from the start."

"Your intuition is finally coming around to the face value of your situation, Yankee, my friend," BP replied. "After all, it isn't every day a young man is visited by a frog, or an ape, or an angel for that matter. Did you really think my amphibian articulations amounted to one more fun story for you to tell as if bantering with those buddies in the bayou bog? Quick, whack me over the head and be done with me, if you think that's what this gig is all about."

I was stunned for a minute, as if the frog had done the whacking, and it took a moment for my mind to catch up with the thoughts running through my brain. I began to sense my extraordinary experience in a way that made me feel small, like the feeling you get when you open your eyes in the middle of a black night, on the top of a mountain beneath a canopy of stars stretching to the horizon all around you. Suddenly whatever the little frog's purpose was for talking to me, it was as big as life, and I felt very small for the task of understanding it.

After draining the tub, I cleaned up the talcum mess I made of my knapsack. Then I did my best to make a temporary living space with it to get BP through his first night in my home. I promised to build him a suitable habitat the next day, complete with moss, a water bowl, and an adequate supply of food, some mealworms perhaps, or some crickets. He assured me that a single juicy earthworm from the garden would be enough to last him the length of his visitation. That's when I realized my new little green friend didn't intend to stay around forever.

He wasn't a pet. He was a prophet with a message.

As long as I was willing to engage him with genuine dialogue while honestly seeking to understand his meaning, BP was keen and ready to trek the line of his message through our conversations. When I suggested that I should begin to make a record of our conversations for future review, the frog celebrated by hopping so high, I thought he'd hit the ceiling. That's when BP suggested a title for our work...

Amphibian Diaries
A Field Guide for Truth-Seekers

I spent rest of the evening in BP's tutorial, doing my best to understand the frog's formula of the SEARCH for truth. After three hours of teaching and dialogue, his voice sounded as if he had his own version of a *frog in his throat.* All tuckered out, he crawled into the knapsack around midnight. But I was too excited to sleep. I spent the next hour chronicling the things I was learning from the frog. By the time I hit the sack, I felt like I had recorded a compendium of his six principles.

REASON

As BP indicated, his message to me was a code made of the six principles to which his poem referred:

1. The **S**oul with a Hole
2. The **E**xpectation of Good
3. The **A**nswers from Outside the Box
4. The **R**eason we trust
5. The **C**orresponding Perception, and
6. The **H**umble Heart

I hope I've already told you enough of my story for you to have a rudimentary understanding of the first three of the six principles he taught.

Truth Principle
The **R**eason we trust.
It is wise to trust reasonable, right, relevant things.

Principle four is the *Reason We Trust*. I could tell the expression of this principle had something to do with our power of reasoning. But BP had a way of teaching things so they would stick. In this case, he told one of his stories to illustrate. He opened with a curious, rhetorical question, born of a bayou fable:

What happened to Fiona Frog?

The story goes that Fiona Frog always wanted to be a mother. But no matter how hard she tried, she could not produce a tadpole. So when she found the baby alligator (he swam so much like a tadpole, and his eyes looked so much like her own, only sadder—like the eyes of a poor puppy in need of a mommy) she was pleased to take him home to her pad and raise him as her son. She called him Terry. Fiona Frog was a very good mother. She fed Terry three square meals a day. But eventually Terry became so large that Fiona could not find enough flies and crickets and other insects to fill his belly. It wasn't long before Terry had Fiona for dinner. And it wasn't long after that when everyone in the pond wondered as to the whereabouts of Fiona Frog. "Where did Fiona Frog go?" "Should we ask her son, or in-Terry-gator?"

"Whatever the case," explained BP, "the moral of the story is this: it is always better to presume reality than to be consumed by it."

Don't worry if the meaning of BP's fable isn't readily obvious to you. It wasn't to me, either. The first purpose of the frog, after all, was to get us *thinking*. So I'll share with you what he shared with me to give you a deeper understanding.

The reality of some things is difficult to identify or understand. When you think about it, most things in the reality of our universe are beyond our understanding. We are very limited in this sense. But the reality of a thing, of any thing, is not limited to how we understand it. BP was very animated about this.

"Reality *Is*," he said. "Reality does not revolve around our understanding." He insisted that we must give up this arrogant, self-inflated idea of human understanding and existence. "In fact," BP continued, "if our understanding does not revolve around the reality of Reality, we are bound to suffer by our foolishness as sure as Fiona Frog can no longer be found, and Terry is smiling."

Then BP went after that existential illustration they use in every Philosophy, Psych, or Sociology 101 class, when they ask, *"If a tree falls in a forest and no one is around to hear it, does it make a sound?"* The frog chided, "As my great family of frogs around the globe will tell you, the bigger the tree, the more horrible a crashing sound it will make so that any frog would be glad to be so far away as a human who cannot hear it!"

And I see how BP is right. It is unreasonable to believe that the reality of anything is subject to our perception of it, or that sounds depend on our hearing them.

The Three "Faith Filters"

At this point, BP emphasized the importance of our capacity for reasoning. He pointed out that reason is at the heart of anything we know to be true. He wanted me to remember that our faith in understanding anything we believe to be true is always a result of three "Faith Filters" that are operative at all times in our lives. I remember the three filters because BP said our minds use them to *"Reason Up"* to a confident understanding of any reality of life.

If we say we know anything to be true about reality, it is because our understanding *Lines Up, Measures Up,* and *Lives Up.* These are the three Faith Filters with which we *reason up* our lives. We use them to gain a sense of surety of the way we understand our lives.

By *lining up*, BP was referring to our natural ability to be logical. You and I know things to be true, in part because we think of things as logically consistent with our experience of them. They *line up reasonably.*

By *measuring up*, BP was referring to the innate tendency that all of us share, experiencing life by a form of scientific method. In other words, BP said, "We know things to be true because we experience their empirical adequacy. *They add up the same each time."*

When BP said the third filter helped us know that our thinking is *living up* to reality, he simply meant that our experience bears out practically and relevantly in our everyday life. We constantly use these three filters to make our way through life with confidence. Without these, we have no level of surety about anything.

Is that clear as mud? Sorry. That's the way it was for me the first time, also. Then BP explained his meaning by way of negative examples, and it all became clearer. I'll tell you the way he told me.

"Let's say I tell you something I believe to be true… whatever, anything, that I might claim is a reality of life. When you hear it—whatever it is—you say to me, 'That is completely unreasonable. It makes no logical sense whatsoever.' And then I say to you, 'I know that it's unreasonable or illogical, but I believe it to be true.' What would you think of me, my belief, and my truth claim? That's right. You would tell me I am *nuts* and that *my thinking is absurd*...because my thinking does not *Line Up* with any point of reason in terms of our ability to make sense of life. That's Faith Filter One.

"Faith Filter Two. Let's say I tell you this is what I believe, whatever, anything I may claim is a reality of life. And when you hear this you say to me, 'That is completely unfounded, and there are five scientific laws of proof that contradict what you believe as true.' And then I say to you, 'I know what I'm saying is unscientific and runs against all evidence, but I believe it anyway!' That's right. You would tell me I am *nuts* and that *my thinking is absurd*...because my thinking does not *Measure Up* to any point that has proven to be true.

"Then Faith Filter Three: Let's say I tell you this is what I believe, whatever, anything I may claim is a reality of life. And when you hear it, you say to me, 'That has never born out in anyone's experience and accomplishes nothing good. In fact, it always goes wrong.' And then I say to you, 'I know what I'm saying doesn't work in life, but I believe it anyway!' That's right. You would tell me I am *nuts* and that *my thinking is absurd*...because my thinking does not *Live Up* to any practical or relevant experience and never goes that way in real life."

Does BP's fourth point of *the Reason We Trust* start to make sense when we look at it expressed like this? The three Faith Filters are innate. They are the way we naturally go about being sure of anything. The reason we trust certain things to be true, and the level of trust we assign to anything we believe to be true, is always an effect of these three ways we think through life, about everything, and at all times.

When you think about it long enough, his point becomes as obvious as the nose on our face. Yet current culture would have us think there is no way to know a truth as an absolute.

BP smiled. "The funny thing is," he said, "you have yourselves absolutely believing there are no absolutes, and end up cutting off your nose to spite the reality of your own face."

CORRESPONDENCE

Two frogs sat on a steel rail. They both felt a vibrating rumble, and the first frog said, "It is a thunderstorm approaching."

The other said, "It is a train."

Then they heard a toot, toot *and the first frog said, "It is the wind."*

The other said again, "It is a train."

Then they saw billowing black smoke approaching. The first frog said, "Here comes the rain cloud."

The second frog said a third time, "It is a train."

A moment later, the second frog jumped off the rail. What hit the first frog?

Reality!

When BP told me this story, I found it humorous. But I didn't get the point as the fifth part of his code. Then I thought about it for a while, and compared it to the way many of my college professors taught about life. They were proud to make a point of saying that we have become a culture that is no longer influenced by the rigid notion of truth as an absolute. I wanted BP to hear it for himself, so I invited him to class with me one day.

To be honest, I had another reason, also. I confessed it on the way to the lecture. "There's a girl who sits next to me in the class."

"What of her?" I heard him ask from within the backpack. He was brusque but curious.

"Well," I responded with hesitation, knowing I would have to be persuasive, "I was wondering if you might work some of your...*magic* on her."

"Magic?" BP jumped.

"Yeah. You know, like the story of the frog prince!"

"You want me to *kiss* her!?" He was clearly disgusted. "Have you any idea of the many dangerous microbes that *princess* carries around in her mouth?"

"No," I snapped back, "I don't want you to *kiss her*!" (Truth is, I was the one who was dreaming of a kiss.) "And *you're* the one with the threat of *salmonella*!"

"Salmonella—howmanila!" he defended. "One in a million of my good frog friends carries salmonella. Besides, you've already given me a bath. How many frogs could admit to that?"

I felt like I was testing his tolerance, and we were nearly to the class. "I don't want you to *kiss* her," I reiterated. "I thought you might simply...say *something* to her."

"*Say* something to her?"

"Yeah. Like, 'Hello, gorgeous!'"

"*Well...*" BP was condescending now. "Keep in mind the truth of thoughts, my friend. They're often a completely different category from reality!"

"What do you mean?" I asked.

"*I mean, she won't...hear me*, at least not as you do," the frog emphasized.

We entered the classroom. There were people all around. So I whispered one last word loud enough for BP to hear my stubborn presumption. "She'll hear you the same as me. Just wait for my sign."

Ten minutes into the lecture, the class was quiet and semi-focused on the professor. I caught her eyes and she smiled in my direction. The timing was perfect. I squeezed my knapsack, signaling BP. I was glad to see him respond. He crawled from the bag and hid himself there between us so that only the *princess* could see him.

"Hello, gorgeous!" He said it just as I asked, to my pleasure. But that's not what she heard.

What she heard was, "Ribbit, ribbit!"

Her smile fell away in an instant. Then she looked at me and said in quiet protest, "Those things carry salmonella!"

I looked at BP, eyebrows raised, as if to say, *Told you so!*

BP looked at me through narrow eyes, as if to reply, *No. I told YOU so!*

(That would be the last time the girl ever looked my way. When next the class met, she was sure to take a seat across the room from me. So much for magic, the princess, and a dream of a kiss.)

We were back to BP's agenda. He quietly instructed through gritted teeth, "Do you think we might return to our reason for being here? Would you kindly focus on the professor's lecture. And please, follow *my* lead this time."

It didn't take long. The professor was talking about

what he called the *anthropological diversity of cultural relativism.* He was very certain of what he was teaching and deliberate with his terms. It was this sentence that caught BP's attention: the professor said, "Of course we all understand there is no such thing as an absolute truth." He said it as though we should all know to agree with him.

"Promptly, raise your hand," BP whispered, "and when the man calls you, repeat *what I say*!"

I did my best to synch with the frog. The man looked at me with my hand in the air and nodded, indicating permission to speak.

"*What I say—what I say*," I repeated.

All of a sudden, the prof and the frog and I were caught in a literal loop of loony-tune puzzlement.

"No, no, NO!" said BP.

"*No, no, NO!*" I parroted.

The class went silent, and the professor was confused. "*What are you saying*, young man?"

BP was frustrated, "Say, 'As the professor said!'"

"As the professor said," I repeated, and the man just stood there looking at me as if I had just landed from planet screwball.

In the next few seconds, BP quickly shut me up, explained his meaning, and reset my objective, reminding me of our earlier conversation.

The class was polite, quietly waiting, but for a few snickers. Embarrassed, I glanced at princess. Wide eyed, she actually scooted her desk away from me.

"I got it!" I responded out loud, in spite of myself.

"I *hope* you do, young man. You are wasting precious class time," he pressed. "What's on your mind, please?"

I was trembling, but finally on track for making the frog's point. "Well, sir," BP whispered.

Then I said out loud, "You said there is no such thing as an absolute."

"That's right!" he confirmed. "I'm glad we're in the same room now."

Several people laughed. I deserved it.

"Uhhh...here's my question then." Straight from BP I repeated it word for word. "Are you *absolutely sure* there are no absolutes?"

It had a stunning effect on the class. I was sure they didn't expect anything so intelligent coming out of *my* mouth. Then someone hooted, and a few laughs wafted in from the front this time.

The professor huffed and stubbornly smiled. "I think I get your drift." He was placating. "But surely you can't be so intolerantly rigid as to suggest that there is an absolute standard for morals in this material world of diverse cultures? I submit there can't be!" he said, throwing his words at me confidently.

I admit, had BP not been there, coaching me, I would not have known how to respond to the man. His presumption seemed so obvious and universally acceptable in my circles. I was initially afraid to respond.

Then I heard BP Frog whisper his wisdom from inside my backpack. I repeated, "Professor, if you were living in Nazi Germany during World War II, *would you rather* be a member of the gestapo or a member of the Jewish culture?"

The room went dead silent.

The professor sneered, "What are you getting at?"

"Well…" BP's words, "were the Nazis wrong to exterminate seven million Jews in the concentration camps, or were they merely expressing a different morality that wasn't ultimately, absolutely wrong?"

The class was only silent for as long as it took the meaning to sink in. Then they started to laugh again, and there was much hooting. The professor didn't even smile. It was uncomfortable for a few seconds, then the bell rang and we were released from class.

On the way home and back at my apartment, BP and I replayed the experience. First we laughed till we cried about the "Who's On First?" debacle of dialogue in the classroom. (Yes, frogs can cry.) Then we reran the entire episode with the professor.

BP showed me how he was caught in a logical fallacy called a *category mistake*. He was confusing two categories: the one we call "reality," and the one we should think of as our "perception" of reality.

BP explained, "The dominant view of the culture today is that *the world is what we make of it, that our perceptions are the reality of our existence.* This is at the center of the social thinking, which claims to be postmodern. That view of life leads to *the postmortem of human reasoning.* Or said another way, according to old G.K.C.,[4] *there is a thought that stops thought, and that is the only thought that ought to be stopped!*"

---

[4] *G.K. Chesterton, that is!*

And that's why BP wanted me to understand the error of a logical, category mistake. It helped for understanding the fifth principle of the SEARCH code,

Truth Principle
5 The Corresponding perception.
We're wise when our ideas and reality agree.

"Did you know," BP asked, "that most frogs and other animals are envious of humans' ability to think so deeply? Animals can think at one level only, *instinctively*. They can't think about *what they think about* as you and I are now."

He pointed out that as we grow and mature into full humans, we naturally learn to be conscious or aware of our way of thinking. We have the amazing ability to make judgments about our judgments of life.

So the frog on the rail in BP's fable is not really so dumb as he is limited to know enough about the world in order to distinguish the reality of the difference between a storm and a steam engine. The irony of the fable is that the other frog is smarter than our current culture, unconscious of the difference between a perception of reality and reality itself, and therefore unable to acknowledge and act upon the difference between a perception that is true to reality and one that is tragically false about reality. In other words, this fifth principle of BP's teaching reminds us that reality is one thing, and our perception another. They are two categories that should not be confused.

BP reminded, "A famous man once said, 'It depends on

the meaning of what *Is*, is.'"[5] The man was playing with people's minds and dancing around a category mistake." He chided with irony, "People used to call *that* infidelity!"

BP had me slow down and think about this until I understood it: the reality of "Is," is not the same as our "perception or thought of what *is*." And whatever it "Is" in reality, our "thoughts of what *is*" will not change *it*. In other words, if our "perception or thinking of what is" is not faithful to what "Is *in reality*," then our perception or thinking is not true, not right, it *Is* wrong...*really!*

Our thinking about *what reality is* does not make it what *it Is*. Killing millions of Jews *Is* murder whether you *think it is* a solution or genocide. The first frog on the rail *Is* a pancake no matter how he interpreted what the approaching rumble *is*. If we can't distinguish between the categories of reality and perception, or if we somehow insist they are one and the same, then how will we avoid being squashed by the next *holocaust* when it is perceived as a *holy cause*?

BP insisted, "If we are going to genuinely SEARCH for truth, then we must understand this principle and be *Conscious of the Corresponding Perception* that is in our minds."

And above all, we must commit to the last principle that BP shared with me.

---

[5]   A reference to the statement made by Bill Clinton during questioning regarding the Monica Lewinski affair.

HUMILITY

I don't want you to think that all my time with BP was spent talking and writing, like a student and teacher in a 24/7 classroom, or a lab. *Life* was BP's classroom. My experience with him was a living lab. It was much more fun than anything I experienced inside the four walls of an educational facility. BP said that *learning and living should be synonymous*, and that one cannot be expected to be full and true without the other.

Getting me to think critically about my thinking of life was a primary objective of BP's visit. And he said that *the best thinking about life was born of experiencing it*. Nearly everything he said, especially the principles he wanted me to remember, grew out of some experience we had together. Sometimes it was clear that the event was custom made by BP to illustrate his point. But usually, the occasions of his teachings were attached to the serendipitous encounters we shared together. It was as if he had all of his wisdom sorted into categories, waiting for just the right experience to come along to serve as an illustration of his point. He claimed in this way there were no coincidences in the human interactions of life because each incident could be a "teachable moment" for a person in SEARCH for Truth.

I figured differently at the start. I thought that it's not every day that a guy meets a talking frog. So I concluded that we should spend as much time together as possible; in my apartment, my face in his, listening and recording his every word. So that's the way we spent the first part of our time together. Then BP put me on to his theory about living and learning. Eventually I resumed my regular schedule. And he insisted on going with me wherever I went. "The only thing worse than sitting through hours of contrived classroom teaching," BP would say, "is missing a teachable moment with your student when they walk through it outside the walls of the classroom!"

That's why and how BP was with me when my friend, Joe Valentino, invited me to watch his son run in the Special Olympics. BP insisted I go rather than stay with him. And he insisted I take him rather than leave him. I'm glad he did.

————————

Joe was a coach for the Special Olympians, so I stood with him, down on the field during the races. BP had full view of everything from within my lapel pocket where I hid him from the rest of the crowd. Joe didn't even notice him there, beneath my windbreaker.

When it came time for his son's race, Joe positioned himself beyond the end of the race and aimed his video camera through the finish line and back at the other end of the track where the 100-meter dash was about to start. The runners were standing by their starting blocks, his son Josh in the middle lane.

BP worked his way up my shirt pocket. Stretching, he was peering out through the zipper opening of my jacket to take in the race. He was fascinated by all the attention that was given to the winner of each race. When it came time for Joe's son's race, BP said something about how nice a view my friend, Josh's father, must have had via the zoom function in his viewfinder.

We could hear the official at the starting line as he gave the first command, calling the runners to their marks, and we watched as Josh and the other runners folded into their starting blocks. When the starter called out, "Now set," we watched Josh raise with the other competitors for a single second to the set position. Then there was a white puff, and a split second later we heard the sound of the starter's gun. We watched as Josh was off with an excellent start. He seemed to press out of the blocks before everyone.

His father predicted this earlier, telling me, "He's usually first out with those lightning-fast reflexes of his." Joe smiled as a father should, the glint of his dark Italian eyes punctuating his joy. I had read in the papers of Josh's string of victories qualifying him to run in this championship race. So I shared his anticipation of victory.

Still, I knew all these kids had worked hard to get to this race. It was evident in the first couple of steps that Josh was clearly faster than the other kids out of the starting blocks. But I also knew that the biggest races bring out the best in good runners. So like everyone else, I was glued to the race to witness the outcomes of the kids' twelve-second opportunity for the thrill of glory, which for nine other runners would be—as *ABC Sports* so famously coined it—the "agony of defeat."

Joe said he often talked to Josh about the race during the last several weeks in the morning before school at breakfast and at night during bedtime. It was the centerpiece of their conversations. They talked about that *great feeling*, to be the first person to cross the finish line, *winning the race*—something to which Josh was getting accustomed.

But I knew from my own experience as a runner, and I whispered my concern to BP in my pocket, "No race is won until it's confirmed by the officials."

"Or that *Accu-Track* finish line photo!" agreed BP.

I'll admit, Joe's confidence in his son's abilities was huge, and it had me a bit concerned as to the outcome. That's one of the things that makes sports and athletic competition so universally popular. The fans know that anything can happen. *It ain't over till it's over.*

In the first ten meters, Josh did have a confident lead that bode well for the next ninety meters. Halfway through, he commanded a monster lead of fifteen to twenty meters. He was crushing the field. It seemed clear to everyone, he would be the winner. The roar of fans in the stands would have easily carried him the rest of the way to break the tape. Then something happened.

I could tell Joe noticed it, too, as he watched through his camera lens. There was concern on his face as Josh reached the sixty-meter mark. He was *slowing down*. The crowd saw it, also. The cheering turned to urging. "Go, Josh… Keep going, Josh!"

Joe left the camera running on its tripod and stepped to its side to make a father/coach's plea. "Keep running, Josh…finish the race. Son, all the way to the finish line, Josh!"

What was wrong? Couldn't Josh hear them? What was he thinking? Josh was still smiling that *life-is-good* smile of his, so everyone knew he wasn't hurt, as if he'd pulled a hamstring or something. Yet clearly, even Joe could see it from his perpendicular perspective at the finish line, Josh was slowing down. By seventy meters he had slowed to a walk. At eighty meters Josh came to a complete stop. And for a brief second, so did the roar of the concerned crowd and the coaching of the completely frustrated father.

As if members of a studio audience reading their cue card, the white noise in the background dialed down just long enough for everyone to hear while they watched Josh turn himself around to face the other runners trailing so far behind him. Then cupping one hand to his mouth, with the other waving them in, Josh called to his friends, "Come on guys!"

As the other runners caught up to him, Josh swung back around to face the finish line with them, then hung his arms around the runners in the lanes on either side of him. The rest of the runners in the other lanes followed his lead. Then, all together—some old friends and teammates, others new friends and would-be competitors, all buddies, *now together*—finished the race, crossed the line, and broke the tape as *one*.

The crowd faded into the background where ordinary things belong. Then, *as if they were a single person who in that moment encountered some sort of unexpected miracle*, they began to cheer all the louder for the strange victory they just witnessed, which was magnified by an automatic wetness in every eye. Joe and I just looked at each other through tears and smiles.

No words were adequate.

Joe laughed. "Wow... that really got your heart pounding, huh?"

I thought about the obviousness of his statement for a brief second, then I noticed how extra hard it seemed my heart *really was pounding*. I realized it was BP kicking and leaping in my pocket and beneath my windbreaker. It must have made for a strange effect to anyone, like Joe, who might have seen it, as if my chest were impregnated by an alien. BP was beside himself, and about to blow his cover. Still, he wouldn't stop his frantic movements. Clearly he was excited about something, and he couldn't wait to tell me.

I moved to a quiet spot behind the stadium bleachers where we could find a private moment together. There, away from the din of the fans of the Special Olympics, I realized how much noise BP was making from inside my pocket. Had we been anywhere else, he would have drawn a lot of attention. He kept croaking, "Did you see that? *Did you see that?*"

I assured him I did, and I said something about it being *very touching*, and a special race, one I was glad I hadn't missed.

"Touching?" BP was beside himself. "What an understatement! I suppose you couldn't help but see it, but do you realize *what* you've seen? A special race, a unique experience, indeed! We've just seen something spectacular in the way that Josh ran his race, so that my final point to you has been illustrated in very real and actual terms!"

Truth Principle
The **H**umble heart.
We learn wisdom from others, with others.

Like a good teacher, BP reiterated his point until he made his intended impression. "The natural perspective that one learns of one's self is too large!" he said. "People will not SEARCH if they are not appropriately small. For when they are in tune with their heart of hearts, they are most able to hear a 'still, small voice inside of them.'"

He went on to make the connection to the code for me and said, "It is the awareness of the hole in one's **S**oul that **E**xpects to be filled with the good life. Then seeking **A**nswers, we learn how *small* we are inside the Box, where we all must live by faith in response to the most critical questions of life. We learn we are not so large as we think we are. In fact, we learn that we are so small, we must **R**each up in our thinking, in search of a life perspective that will *Line Up, Measure Up,* and *Live Up to the truth* in a way that **C**orresponds to reality. Yankee, if this formula I have been sharing with you is ever to bear the fruit of hope and joy that each soul seeks, then to finish the honest seeker's code. Above all, in all this, you must be **H**umble. S-E-A-R-C, and H, is the Humility required to be a genuine truth-seeker."

BP emphasized, "I said it before and I'll say it again, especially now by way of young Joshua Valentino's graphic illustration. The search for the truth is humble to whole, for purposeful life and peace for the soul!"

That last line from the frog's code of principles sounded

beautiful to me even the first time I heard it. But by the time BP and I arrived home from the Special Olympics event, it was really bugging me, because I had no idea what it meant!

A Point

Back at my apartment, I rolled the last line of the code over and over in my head…

The search for truth is humble to whole,
For purposeful life and peace for the soul.

I was missing something, and BP knew it. No sooner did I remove my jacket when he leapt from my chest pocket to my bed in a single grand hop, then perched himself on my pillow at the headboard. I made my own dive to the bed and the box springs recoiled, whining with disapproval as I bounced to prone in front of the frog. We were level to each other, eyeball to eyeball.

"Tell me more about humility and this last line of the code," I asked.

"Yes, we need to give special focus to this one," said the frog, "for there are as many as three dimensions to its meaning for you to understand. And you must understand humility if you are going to recognize the truth of anything."

"Three dimensions?" I reiterated.

"Yes," BP confirmed, "*dimensions of humility*, like in geometry: a point, a line, a cube."

"Wait!" I caught myself. "Press the pause button, Mr. Frog. I can tell I'm going to need to write this down."

The frog was clearly pleased, and willing to wait a moment while I collected my journal and pencil. I repositioned myself, legs folded, Indian-style directly in front of my green teacher.

There was a sparkle in BP's eyes. He was pumped that night. I thought it was because he was still riding the high from Josh's race, or because of the subject matter. Later, as I looked back on it, I realized it was because he knew it was his last evening with me. He was excited with the anticipation of finishing my lessons so that he could release me to the purpose of Andy's invitation, which still remained unopened.

"The first essential dimension of genuine humility," BP began, "is *intra*personal."

"In-*ter*-personal?" I asked, thinking he had misspoken.

"No," he said, "In*ter*personal is the second dimension, which has to do with the relationship between persons. In*tra*personal is the first dimension, and has to do with a person's relationship to their self. That is why it is represented by a single point in this spiritual form of geometry."

The look on my face insinuated my lack of understanding.

BP expanded his explanation. "Every individual is the point," he said. "Inside each point, in each person, there is a constant conversation. For example, at this very moment, you are taking in what I say and thinking about it to yourself...*with yourself.* Inside your person, somewhere in your head I suppose, or perhaps between your head and your heart, or your heart and your soul, you repeat to yourself the words I just said. Then another part of you responds, asking, 'What do I think of BP's statement?' You evaluate my statement, affirming some level of understanding while deciding whether or not you believe my statement to be true. It is an in-*tra*-personal conversation, when you are aware of it."

I was catching on. "I think someone has called it 'self-talk.'"

"Very good, dear Yankee. You've indeed nailed it. The intrapersonal aspect of humility focuses on 'self-talk.' In that conversation, *by* self-talk, inside your head, you process all of your experiences, and come to know your life, your *self* by way of *interpretation*. We've been talking about this all along, haven't we, Yankee?"

As he said it, it was dawning on me. Everything we'd discussed to that point—the entire code and the SEARCH for Truth—had something to do with understanding this intrapersonal dimension to which BP was referring. "The hole in the Soul is *my* voice, someplace deep inside me, searching," I said like a reflex, "and every decision I make—conscious or unconscious—I make in response to *my* voice, Expecting good to come of my choices." I was on a roll. "If I think about it, there is a constant conversation inside me revolving around the Answers I'm seeking to the critical questions of life, which can only be answered by faith. Reasoning; that's certainly the business of self-talk as I decide whether the voices in my head *Line Up*, *Measure Up*, and *Live Up* to the truth. And the entire conversation is a constant check of my perspective—or the way I see things, as if I'm constantly asking myself, 'Does my way of thinking Correspond to reality?'"

BP urged me on, hoping I'd made the final connection. "And what of 'H'?"

"I think I see, BP," I continued. "Humility seems to be the attitude required of a person who is a Truth-Seeker."

"I'm proud of you," he said. "I think you're understanding the intrapersonal aspect of the process, the first dimension of humility. True Truth-Seekers have a humble attitude about them, which causes them to constantly think about their thinking, to be aware of their *interpretations* of life."

For the next couple minutes, BP drilled down into this idea of interpretation. He said the understanding of it was essential to forming my attitude of humility, and the link from his first point to the next—or the *line*, which is the second essential dimension of humility. Once he finished this micro-teaching, I asked him to repeat himself, slowly, that I might transcribe it. The following is straight from the mouth of the frog, pure BP.

A Line

Start of Transcription

Interpretation is a critical human activity, which constantly occupies our thinking, because we interpret everything in life. It is a sensitive subject because it is subjective. Interpretation is a judgment, and our judgments are always subjective—limited by our capacity to know anything inside the Box.

This would be a small problem in a world of one person, or a world of perfect people. But we live with others on this planet, lots of others, and none of us is perfect. The paths of our lives constantly cross. We bring our interpretations with us into those intersections. This makes interpretation a subject with potential for great harm. The personal limits of our knowledge are often the source of our conflict.

This leads to the importance of *interpersonal* humility. Humility, among other things, is the recognition of our limits. It is a choice we all must make. Since no one possesses perfect, complete knowledge, interpretation requires humility. We must be able to admit we are not the Source or the Sustainer of our existence. We are not capable of complete interpretations or perfect judgments of anything. No one person can depend on themselves for complete and correct understanding of anything. When we come to this understanding of ourselves, we are ready to choose humility in relationship with others *interpersonally*.

Understanding the singular, lonely point of our existence, we are ready, postured for the potential of other people...other points to which we connect and form lines, the second dimension. We're ready to acknowledge our importance to each other for a more complete view of anything. The interpersonal, second dimension of humility.

We need each other for a check on the sense of assurance that our perceptions correspond to the truth of reality. Our tendency to self-reliance has great potential for self-deception, as if *somehow*, the truth of anything is *defined by us* rather than *discovered by us*. That way of thinking is most dangerous for all parties involved. Consider the story of the Blind Frogs.

One blind frog sat on the tail of the alligator, thinking to himself, *It is the trunk of an elephant.* So he struck up a conversation with his presumed friend. Another blind frog sat on the leg of the alligator and thought, *This is the root of a tree.* So he rested there a while. The third blind frog found his way to the alligator's smile, his teeth completely exposed. The frog thought, *What a neat wall of rocks I've found.* A moment later, that frog had second thoughts about the wall when they suddenly separated and exposed sharp edges.

That's when I called to the blind frogs to warn them. "Alligator," I cried as loud as I could.

Just as I did, the fourth blind frog found the alligator's mouth wide open, saying, "I've found a hallow log to hide in."

The next thing I knew, the other three frogs followed the voice of the fourth straight into that presumed safe hole. And no one ever heard from the four blind frogs again.

If only the frogs could have been reconciled to the limits of their senses, which put them in such precariousness.

Maybe then they could have learned the humble power of friendship. As colleagues, working together, they could have compared the notes of their limited observations to the bigger picture, produced by their combined discoveries. Perhaps then one of those blind frogs might be telling you this story instead of me.

End of Transcription

BP insisted that I give my pencil a rest. "I've heard myself talking too much," he said. "I need to hear from you. It's important for me to get a sense that you're understanding me, especially if you're going to be sharing my words with others. Anyone can write words, Yankee, but few understand their meaning, and even fewer can move that meaning on to other minds."

I wanted to impress him. "I think what you mean is that *intra*personal understanding is difficult, and *inter*personal understanding even harder."

BP smiled and snorted a short frog laugh. "Okay, wise Yankee, go on."

I explained, "Well, the first dimension of intrapersonal humility is admitting personal limitations. Each of us needs to recognize that our understanding of things is bound in the Box by our short life of experience."

"Go on..." he urged with an encouraging smile.

"Yes," I added, "that's just the first point, or dimension. The other point makes a line and the second dimension of humility. We need each other. A single truth-seeker has trouble enough. But if two truth-seekers would work together, interpersonally, they can bring their perspectives together, talk of them, and compare them. And if they work at it, they can broaden their combined and personal perspectives."

"That's right!" BP confirmed. "Two truth-seekers—if they are genuine and humble—can be a great help to each other—"

"Four eyes on the gator would have been better than two, even if they *were* blind, as long as they were willing to work together for the sake of each other!" I interrupted.

"Very good," laughed the frog.

"Yet there is more, a third dimension you mentioned," I prodded.

"That's right." He laughed again. "We're ready for it now."

A Cube

I had a question to segue the discussion to the third dimension of humility. "I've been thinking about what you might mean by the next dimension. I see a three dimensional cube in my mind, and it looks a lot like a box."

"*And?*" BP urged me on.

"*And* I wonder if *the Box* we spoke of earlier and this cube have anything in common."

"Excellent, Yankee, my friend," he responded. "I can't tell you how much it means to me when you do such fine *intrapersonal* thinking about our thinking. Now we may put our humble minds together for more thinking about a cube and a box in the *interpersonal* sense, pushing out and beyond ourselves, if you will."

"But we can only go so far," I reminded him.

"I believe you're making a connection. Go on."

"As we go about our lives, the Box contains us. We're naturally limited by it. We can only go so far in our thinking—"

"Even together, interpersonally?" BP interjected.

"Yes, I suppose that's true. We're both limited by the Box."

"Yet," he tested, "there is no denying the Box exists. We can agree on that, can we not?"

"Yes," I concurred. "Though there's no way of certainly knowing *how* it came to exist, or how we came to exist in it. As you've said, that is a matter of faith for us all."

"You are right, Yankee. You have been listening and learning well. But let me ask you something. Is it possible that someone exists *beyond* the Box?"

I thought for a moment. "Why, yes, I suppose. You're referring to the supernatural. In other words, that would be Someone like God!"

"Yes, that would be...*supernatural*...*God*. Interesting, you invoke the term *supernatural*. What do you mean by this in relation to the Box?"

"Well," I answered, "if there is a God, or a Someone beyond the Box, then God is beyond anything we know as natural *in* the Box. In other words, God is *supernatural*."

"I agree," said the frog. "God would be *beyond* natural. So what does this say about God in relation to us and the Box."

This is where I got stuck. I needed BP to open my mind to his implication. He extended his legs and pulled himself from off my pillow and onto my journal. "Would you please lend me your pencil for a moment?" he asked.

"It's all yours," I responded. It was funny to see the pencil in his hands, more like a tent pole in comparison to his size. He used both hands to maneuver it. Clumsy as he looked, his drawings were decent. I've included his work here.

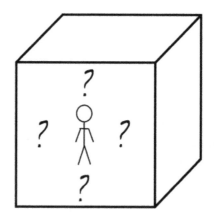

First he drew a box. Clearly it represented *the* Box we'd been talking about from the start. He drew a stick figure of a man inside the Box to represent all of us. He also drew four question marks in the Box.

I followed BP's lead. "That's our Box with humankind stuck inside. I would imagine the four question marks represent our ultimate questions, which can only be answered by faith."

"Very good," he continued, "and where are the answers to our ultimate questions in relation to the Box?"

"Beyond the Box," I replied.

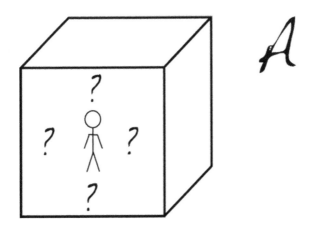

The frog complemented me as he drew an "A" outside the Box. "Excellent. This 'A' will represent all the answers to our ultimate questions of life, answers that are beyond our natural ability to answer. Now we said God is supernatural. Where would you put a 'G' to represent God's nature."

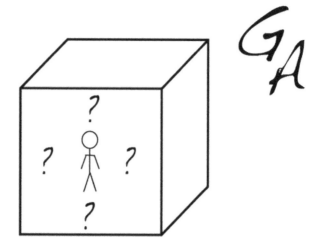

That seemed obvious. So I made a "G" outside the Box, also. As I did, I realized where BP was going with this diagram. "God being supernatural is beyond the Box, not bound by the limits that naturally constrain us!"

BP smiled gently with eyes closed, clearly enjoying my answer. "And, *pray tell*, what is the point of my illustration?"

"Well," I said, "I think you're making a statement. If both our answers and God exist beyond the Box, then it stands to reason that a supernatural God knows the answers to our questions that we naturally can't answer!"

"Yes, dear Yankee," he agreed, "and that would lead to the possibility of great hope for us, especially if God cares for us and loves us. You see, we can't get beyond the Box—"

The lights went on and I finished his sentence, "But a

supernatural God could certainly come to us from beyond the Box! Getting into the Box, bringing the answers *to* us would be a piece of cake for God."[6]

"That's right," said the frog, "and with that, you have invoked the third dimension of humility. We will call it the *inspirational* dimension."

"Wait!" I threw up my hands. "I'm pretty sure I know how you mean that term, but I need a dictionary to make sure. That app came with my phone." I pulled it from my pocket, swiped the screen, tapped the app, the technology popped to life, and I input the spelling as BP barked it out, letter for letter.

"I-n-s-p-i-r-a-t-i-o-n."

In an instant, the definition was in front of me. I zeroed in on the primary meaning and read it aloud, "'A divine influence or action on a person, qualifying them to receive and communicate sacred revelation.'

"Give me one more second..." I wasn't sure about that last term, *revelation*, either. So I tapped on it to show its meaning. "It says, 'a: an act of revealing or communicating divine truth, b: something that is revealed by God to humans.'"

"Yes," responded BP. "This gets at the third level or dimension of humility. The first, the *intrapersonal* dimension, has to do with the personal communication inside one's head. The *interpersonal* dimension of humility pertains to the interaction between persons. And the *inspirational*

---

6   The philosopher's problem of transcendence is answered by the condescendence of the God that cares.

dimension explains the potential for connection between humans and a supernatural being such as God.

"In other words, as we've said," BP extrapolated, "a humble soul *lives life by faith as a bet in the answers they believe to the Four Ultimate Questions.* And a humble soul also knows it is entirely possible for God to know the truth of those answers, and to make the truth known to us in the Box, by *inspiration.*"

I don't know why I found this troubling, but I did. I think I was concerned about the implication. My immediate *intra*personal thought was that he might be talking about *the Bible.* It was an ancient book, and I considered it outdated. I decided, since we had been talking about the humble need of *inter*personal openness for checking our thoughts, that I should voice my concern with my little friend. "It sounds like you're leading to say something about *the Bible.*"

"And what if I was?" he asked with a smirk.

"Well, it's just that I know it is a very old book, and I can't see how something written so long ago can have meaning for us today."

"I think you're making a valid challenge. So what have you learned by looking into your challenge? How did the Bible check out?" He was still smirking.

He'd caught me. I'd never cracked the book. I didn't even have a copy in the apartment. Now I was smirking, and my silence said it all.

"Don't feel bad. There are many like you," he said. "They have the same opinion of the Book, yet it is an idea that is more informed by the opinion of others than an actual firsthand experience with it."

Then the frog said some things that made a lot of sense, things I'd never considered before. "The Bible *is* very old, as you have suggested," he agreed. "The final chapters of it were written before the end of the first century, nearly 2,000 years ago. The first chapters were written 3,500 years ago, and at least one of the books may be as old as 4,000 years. But I'm surprised the age of the Bible doesn't have a more *positive* effect on your opinion of it."

I didn't understand what he meant, and I told him so.

"First of all," he responded, "perhaps you're forgetting that the Box is something that cuts off all of us from the answers to our ultimate questions of life, not just you, or even your generation. The answers have transcended humans in every generation in all of time."

I could see where BP was going, so I finished his thought. "Wow, sure, that's true. In other words, when we've been saying *each of us is a soul with a hole*, we've been referring to everyone…*in all of time.* I haven't been thinking small enough about myself." It was a cheap way of saying I was lacking humility when it came to this idea of our need for the inspirational dimension. But BP was gentle with me. I could tell by the way he smiled, like a caring father. It was an endearing trait of his.

He capped my thought. "Yes, dear Yankee, whatever the inspiration might be from outside the Box, why wouldn't we expect that supernatural word to be very old? A word that has been bringing hope from the first of written history. In fact, the oldest portions of the Bible were orally passed along for generations before the advent of the technology of the written word. That means it's very possible that this

Supernatural Inspirer that we call God has been revealing the answers our soul most needs from the beginning of our creation. And isn't that what a humble soul might expect of a God who truly cares for us *all?*"

I must admit, as usual, the frog was making sense. But before I had the chance to tell him, he went on to his second point.

"And considered this," the frog continued, "why wouldn't you think of this ancient attribute of the Book as a worthy test of its reliability?"

I told him I wasn't sure what he meant, so he explained.

"From start to finish, it took 1,500 years to complete the Bible. It contains sixty-six books that were written by forty-four authors who are claimed to be inspired by God for revealing the Word to humankind from across three continents, and written in two different languages." He paused.

I still didn't get his point.

"Don't you see?" he asked.

I shook my head.

"It's a grand test," the frog said enthusiastically. "How can you explain all those years, so many and diverse authors, even writing in different languages…yet the Bible presents as a single, harmonious message? The answers it provides to the questions each soul is seeking are so coherent, so cogent, and so current for so many cultures in every generation… How *do* you, how does *anyone*, explain that? There is no other book like it under the sun, never has been, never can be."

I'd never considered this. I was silent. I quietly nodded and smiled.

"At the very least, a humble soul would be *intra*-personally open to the possibility that the One beyond the Box has cared enough for those of us who are naturally bound by it to *communicate* by *inspiration* the answers to life's most important questions—our Origin, Destiny, Meaning, and Morality. And I'm hoping that you, dear Yankee, and those who come after you, will be open to an *inter*personal conversation with someone who might humbly seek those answers with you." He sat there with a wide, knowing grin on his face, chin held high. He waited as if it were my turn to do something. And I knew what it was.

We had covered the entire code for the search, and BP had made his way all the way around and back again to the invitation I'd been given at the start. It was time to open it, and there was no question in my mind that it was what I wanted. I was already nodding in approval. "I'd be a fool if I didn't hop on a chance to check out that invite," I said as I made my way to my knapsack to find it.

"So hop you must, good Yankee, and hop you may," BP responded, "but what do you say we hop on down to the bench by the bay to open it?" He hopped to the bag and jumped in.

I slung the two over my shoulder and made my way for the door. It was an exciting moment, except for the sense that my time with the frog might be ending.

The Invitation

The sun was low at the other end of the bay from our bench. It was directly in our eyes when I sat down and set the knapsack beside me. We had about thirty minutes before the sun would slip into the water to end the day. A million waves melted together and made a sparkle island. Billowy clouds towered from one end of that western sky to the other like a mountainous cathedral for a backdrop. It would be a spectacular sunset. That's what BP promised as he slipped from the sack to my side, the invite between his little green hands. We sat there for a moment and drank it in.

BP croaked. It was a loud belch, which startled me. We both laughed. "Can you translate that? It means, '*open the invite, Yankee...a frog don't have forever!*'" he said with a full-blown Cajun accent reminiscent of Wayne Waggenspack or Roy Robisure.

I howled. It broke the tension, and I was ready. I took the invite from the frog. The envelope still read the same as it had from the start.

An Invitation to...
Conversations about Life & God

I had an idea of what was coming. But I was not sure why it created such trepidation in me. Even after all I'd been through with BP, and even though we sat on our bench where only a few days before that giant cloud as a question mark had hung over us, punctuating my deep soul searching, I was still anxious as I opened the envelope.

I ripped it open. The invite was wrapped in a letter that was clearly meant for me to read before the invite. Andy had carefully gathered his thoughts to make a heartfelt, handwritten introduction.

———

1 By now, we know each other well enough that it shouldn't surprise you, I am a person who believes in God. But there was a time when my life was very different. On the outside it may have looked like I had it all together. But on the inside I was empty and desperately searching for a meaningful life. I couldn't find anything to satisfy the deepest needs of my soul. I was sure of nothing, especially my life, and I had no idea where it was all going.

One day, a good friend asked me if I would consider an invitation to a discussion about Life and God. If he was not such a good guy, a real, authentic, nonthreatening type, who seemed to have a handle on life, I probably would have blown him off. And his timing was right. I was searching.

2 I took him up on his invitation and we started meeting together at a coffee shop each week. I threw my deepest, toughest questions at him, especially the stuff that bugged me about God. He didn't judge me. In fact, he admitted that he often faced some of the same challenges. He did his best to respond from a believer's perspective. We also read a book together and discussed it. It was excellent, very thought provoking. It seemed to anticipate many of the issues that challenged us.

It was weeks after our last meeting when something I had read started driving me nuts. A philosopher by the name of Pascal wrote it in a way that stuck with me. He said, Either God is, or he is not. But to which view shall we be inclined? ...A coin is being tossed that will come down heads (God) or tails (no God). How will you wager? It occurred to me that even if I refused to commit one way or the other, I couldn't prevent the coin from being tossed, and it was the same as calling tails.

3 Then I had a close call, one of those experiences that reminds you that you aren't going to live forever. I wrecked my bike. Worse, I really wrecked my body, broken bones all over, and I had to have a hip replaced. While I was lying there on my back, day after day, I had a lot of time for thinking. I was reading another excellent book on the subject of faith when my friend came by to visit. That's when I decided to place my faith in God and to seek Him for answers. I learned about Jesus and all that God did for me through Him. I decided that my best choice was to trust Him as Savior and Lord of my life.

From that day to this, my life has not been the same in every good way imaginable. I have learned my purpose in life, and how, and why I want to live it. I've even got the peace of knowing that the next time I wreck the bike, even if I should lose my life, my future is secure with Him... God promises to take care of me in His forever Love.

As you might imagine, I am very grateful for what I've found with God. I feel like I've been given the antidote to the soul-searching disease that infects all of us. So I'm wondering if you want to join me for a series of weekly discussions like my friend had with me. That's what the invitation is all about. And at least you know a bit more about me and how and why I tick!

If you're not up for it, don't worry. It will not change anything between us. I will always enjoy your friendship. And there will always be a cream puff waiting for you.

You can imagine, after spending the time with BP Frog, I anticipated something like this from Andy. Still it felt a little intrusive. I'm not sure why, but a discussion about God and life still seemed too personal. Then I thought about how I knew Andy. I liked him from the first time I met him. He always felt like an approachable, trustable guy.

I thought about the subject: *God and Life.* Certainly the issues of Origin, Destiny, Meaning, and Morality were the most critical and even inescapable questions of life. I wondered why it should seem to be such an intrusive topic. Where did I get the idea it was such a private thing? What would I risk having a conversation about God? As I thought about that, a deeper question hit me with concern: What would I be risking *if I weren't willing to have the conversation about God and Life?* That's when I decided it was definitely time to check out the invite.

BP Frog smiled with a satisfied grin, ear to ear, as I slipped the card from the envelope.

An invite to join me in a one-on-one discussion
for seeking the reason and relevance of God
and the promise of life in God's Love
that is full of peace and purpose.

The Rules Are Few and Simple:

1. We will meet once a week for seven weeks,
2. At a location that encourages private conversation,
3. For at least an hour in duration,
4. Keeping the discussion to God and Life issues,
5. In a dialogue of openness and understanding,
6. While reading from the list of suggested books,
7. And through it all, maintaining a mindset of…

The Principles of the SEARCH for Truth

Each of us lives as a *Soul with a Hole*,
So we run and run yet fall short of our goal;
We reset the bar, *Expecting the Good*,
Yet never get far as we think we should!

———

Our questions have *Answers* from outside the box
So we live by a faith that guides our thoughts
That wisdom would try by test of *Reason*
In search of good that's right in all season

———

So pry and try the *Corresponding perception*,
And examine each thought by trial of reflection
To search for the truth that's *Humble* and whole
For purposeful life and peace for the soul

The Reading List of Suggested Books

20 Compelling Evidences that God Exists, Second edition.
Ken Boa & Rob Bowman; David C. Cook, 2005

The Case for Christ: *A Journalist's Personal Investigation*
Lee Strobel; Zondervan Publishing House, 1998

The Christ Commission
Og Mandino; Bantam Books, 1983

Discovering God: *Exploring the Possibilities of Faith*
Dennis McCallum; New Paradigm Publishing, 2014

Finding God at Harvard: *Spiritual Journeys of Thinking Christians*
Kelly Monroe; Zondervan Publishing House, 1996

Mere Christianity
C. S. Lewis; Collier Books, 1952

More Than a Carpenter
Josh McDowell; Tyndale House, 1977

Since Nobody's Perfect: **How Good Is Good Enough?**
Andy Stanley; Multnomah Publishers, 2002

Reason for God: *Belief in an Age of Skepticism*
Timothy Keller; Dutton, 2008

There Is a Plan
Ravi Zacharias; Zondervan Publishing House, 2009

Yes or No: *Straight Answers to Tough Questions*
Peter Kreeft; Ignatius Press, 1991

---

*Dear friend: There's no rush or pressure in this invite. It
will remain open to you for whenever you are ready. If
and when you decide you are a "Taker" for the LifeBet,
contact me so we can discuss a time and place for when
and where we can get together for our first meeting!*

Sincerely for truth-seeking with you,

Your LifeBet "Maker"   Andy

The Hop

BP gave me time to read Andy's cover letter, the invite, and plenty of time to think about them, a good fifteen minutes in all. Other than sleeping, it was the longest period of silence I spent in his presence. He was clearly giving me space to consider the offer.

Seven weeks, one hour per week, and a book to read and discuss related to the subject of God and Life. At first, I figured it was like taking a half semester of a college class on a subject that was ten times as important as any I had ever studied. Of course, the unique things about this class were its size and the way we would go about learning our subject matter. I supposed the direction of the dialogue between the two of us would be up to me, primarily. And there would be no quizzes or tests, and no grade. In the end, I decided it was more like a self-guided conversation than a class, and one I was free to lead.

Several questions were already forming in my mind about which I'd always wished I could have talked with somebody. *Why should I believe in a God I've never met or seen? If there is a God who loves us, then why is there so much suffering in the world? Why should I trust the Bible as God's Word about the Truth of Life when there are so many other religious claims?* And, *How can I know what will happen to me and the people I love after we die?* As I thought about how important my questions were in the grand scheme of things, I was glad someone like Andy was making himself available for the conversation. But then, I wondered, would he really be up for it? Did he know what he was getting himself into when he extended this invite to me?

Again, I asked myself what I was worried about. It wasn't as if Andy were some sort of adversary. He'd simply offered to join me in a conversation about God. And it wasn't as if Andy were some sort of spiritual expert about God. He was merely claiming to have found something important about life that he wanted to share with me, and he was clearly going out of his way to protect the conversation for the direction of my need.

I was just about to step into the opportunity when BP Frog anticipated me and spoke first. "If you're going to take up this invitation, then I must make few remaining *humble* suggestions."

I nodded.

BP continued. "Think now and list all the reasons and issues that are in the way of a faith in God so that you can focus on them in the process. You might even give them to Andy in your first meeting so that he can prepare thoughtful responses to your questions and issues. And don't hold back anything. How often do you get this kind of chance in life?"

The frog made another point. "Next, don't attempt this exercise alone. It was always meant to be a shared experience so that one person's perspective may sharpen the other's. And make sure you read together one or more of the books along the way. They were selected from among the best with this exercise in mind. And this way the two of you can learn together from others who have put major time and effort into these issues, rather than putting all the pressure on Andy as if he were some answer man, which I assure you he does not claim to be." He paused.

"Anything else?" I asked.

"One last thing," he replied. "Don't forget to be open to the potential of a Someone beyond the Box. The two of you will need all the help you might be able to get for this discussion. This last suggestion may seem a little odd, but I think it'll make a certain kind of sense. It's just a private thing between you and the God that could be."

"Yes?" This was sounding a little strange, even for the frog, and I was curious.

"Though you may never have done it before, I suggest you be open to *praying* a very simple prayer from a true heart, quietly to yourself, before you start each meeting and perhaps also before your reading."

"A *prayer*?"

"Nothing fancy or formal, just a word or two, as if there were Someone out there who could, somehow, answer you... Consider saying silently to that Someone as if they might be there, '*If You are God, please help me to believe the Truth of You, Your Love and Life.*' I think you can do it," he encouraged. Then with a little smirk, he added, "Unless, of course, you have already decided that you are certain there is no God...no one out there to answer you!"

Honestly, I wasn't sure why, but that was an idea I never would have come up with on my own: *praying*. I don't think I'd ever done it before. I wondered how I would do it and whether I could do it sincerely. Then it occurred to me. If there was a God, He should know what was in my heart and the sincerity of it anyway. So I figured it wouldn't hurt to try it along the way in the process.

While thinking about my heart, I heard my stomach growl. As usual, I was so enthralled in the experience with BP that I had forgotten to eat since early that morning, just before Josh's track meet. I didn't need to look at the time. The big orange ball at the end of the bay had slipped halfway into the water, so I knew it was well past dinner.

"Dinner!" The thought shocked me back to reality. It was already late Monday evening. "Monday!" An entire week had blown by since seeing Andy last when he gave me the invite. Normally—and I mean weekly for three years—I always visited him in the afternoon for my cream puff.

I pulled out my phone and quickly hit the cab company number on my speed dial. I was very worried that Andy might misinterpret my tardiness with respect to the invite.

The dispatcher recognized my number and voice. "I suppose you'll be wanting whichever driver is closest, per usual?" she asked.

"Sure," I said. "Thank you very much."

"He's not five minutes away from you at this very moment."

I was happy to hear her say that. I hung up the phone and turned back to BP Frog. Curiously, though he'd been there between me and the knapsack just a second earlier, that place was empty. I checked the knapsack. I was surprised to find it empty, too. In that moment I heard a *plop* as if someone tossed a stone to the water in front of me, and my stomach sank. When I looked to the water I noticed the rapidly expanding rings in the lily pads about a foot from the shore.

A few seconds later, the ripples were gone. A glasslike dead calm replaced the temporary disruption in the hot, pink sunset shallows of the bay.

Just then, a speedboat pulling a skier came zipping by, ten meters from the shore. The skier sliced in my direction, making rooster tail, clearly attempting to soak me as I sat on the bench. The last of his spray fell short into the water near my feet, in those same lily pads. Thirty meters down the beach, sitting at the next bench on a dock, I heard a fisherman cursing the skier. His seat made him the true victim of the skier's wake. He was soaked.

He cast his bait to the bay futilely, in the direction of the skier as if to snag him. It landed five meters away from me in the water, where the bobber did a couple of major bobs in the final waves of the speedboat and skier. In the next instant, a shadow passed between me and the sunset as a very large bird dove into the water after the fishing line. It was the crane that fished each day along the banks of the bay in front of the apartments.

One, two, three… It all happened just like that, and that fast. I was struck with horror for my little friend. If the skier and the boat hadn't taken him out, then I was concerned that crazy crane had. And if they had missed him, would BP know better than to take the scrumptious worm the fisherman had no doubt baited to the hook on the end of his line?

Honk, honk, honk. The taxi driver arrived. But I hardly noticed. I just sat there frozen in fear for BP the Frog. I don't know how long it was. Long enough that the driver had to honk again. And I was sure I'd seen the last of my little friend. There was nothing I could do. The only thing that was certain in my mind was that BP intended for my visits with him to end, then and there.

"Thanks, little friend!" I said to the bay.

I knew it was over. I was shocked and sad as I walked up to the cab. I didn't even notice the driver who was holding the door for me.

The Intersection

"Hey, didn't I drop you off here last week about this time?" It was TaxiZack. I recognized him as he closed the door behind me and as he circled around the yellow car to his door. I could hardly work up a smile in his direction as he took his place behind the wheel and started to drive away. "Well, you couldn't stop the train so you decided to call a cab?" he joked as he looked at me in the rearview mirror for my reply.

I managed an obligatory chuckle, and told him it was good to see him again. Then I told him I wanted him to take me to the corner of Lane Avenue and Northwest Blvd.

"You headed to *the sausage truck* where we stopped last week?" he asked.

I nodded.

"I think I've stopped there three times since I saw you last. Got a Brat-Mama-Bomba each time. And that Andy is a great guy. Quite the conversationalist. Has a great take on life."

"Yup. That's the truth." I thought about the irony as I said it. And that's all I said. In short time, TaxiZack got the idea: something was up and I didn't feel like visiting this time. The shock of the sudden loss of BP was still dawning on me. But the excitement of the day wasn't over.

A that moment, we passed through a busy intersection within two miles from my home, and just two blocks from where Andy parked his sausage truck. I'd been through that stoplight a thousand times in my life. But there was no light this time, so the corner looked like so many other corners along our way as we passed it. TaxiZack proceeded through the middle and headed east, missing the stop altogether. Friends would find out later that the city had taken down the stoplight for the day to repair it, replacing it with temporary stop signs.

What seemed as several minutes in slow motion happened in a split second. The thing I remembered most was the sound of it. It sounded like a locomotive engine, horn and all, a large red blur racing by the front of the cab. It was a fire engine, northbound, on its way back to station after a false alarm. TaxiZack jerked on the wheel and the front of the car spun to the right, nearly missing the tail end of the truck. I heard a crack. It was the driver's side rear light as it clipped the ladder on the back of the truck.

The cabby's foot was frozen cold to the brake, all the way to the floor. The car turned into a skidding, spinning yellow top, crossing the westbound lane, missing all oncoming traffic as it did one more spin before straightening out. We were headed for the pole on the southeast corner. That's when TaxiZack panicked and took his foot off the brake as he quickly jerked the car one more time, hard to the right. He managed to miss the pole and get the car headed in the direction of a driveway just south of the corner.

The bottom of the car hit hard and scraped on the concrete apron of the driveway, making another awful sound, then bounced and hit the drive again. It seemed like TaxiZack took his foot off the brake. I would find out later that his brakes had given out completely. At this point we were going no faster than five miles an hour, but the front door of the apartment complex on that corner was rapidly approaching.

We were rolling at an angle through the front yard. We missed one pine tree to the right of the car, then TaxiZack steered us past another pine on the left. The branches scraped against the doors of the car, slowing us down. We were nearly crawling as the car rolled over a bush, which caught and stopped us just before the taxi, ever so lightly, bumped the front door of the apartment. In that very second, the occupant of the apartment opened the door and stood there, surprised, mouth wide open. That would have been a safe and fitting ending.

But in the very same second, TaxiZack started screaming. I thought the traumatic event had thrown the poor driver into a heart attack. He lifted the handle to his door and slammed his shoulder into it at the same time. The door swung open, caught on its hinge, and hit the driver on its way back as he was half out of the car.

In the next second, I watched as he started to undo his belt buckle and pull down his pants. TaxiZack reached down his pant leg, screamed one more time, then pulled out his hand, holding something over his head. I turned to see the man in the door one more time, still standing there, mouth opened, now looking at TaxiZack's hand over his head. I looked back with the man at TaxiZack. And there he stood, holding a frog by the legs dangling over his head. He had a crazy look in his eyes.

Slowly, TaxiZack lowered his hand to his side and released the frog to the half of the bush that wasn't under the car. He looked at me. Then ever so slowly rolled his head until his eyes met with the man at the door. He was the first to laugh, just a puff, and a, "Hey, how about that!?"

TaxiZack replied to his puff with another, and responded in kind, "Yup, how about that!?" At that point we roared with laughter. That's how the fireman found us as he made his way from the intersection, through the yard, and to our side.

Two blocks away, Andy in his sausage truck heard the deafening engine horn, the terrible screeching and skidding of our tires, and the earsplitting crack of the car when it hit the drive apron. Sure of a dreadful accident, he automatically ran to the scene to offer what aid he may. He was in such a hurry to help that he was still holding the cream puff he had been serving to his patron in the previous moment. Now he was standing next to the fireman. Both men, jaw dropped, were trying to take in what they were seeing. The look on their faces was enough to keep us laughing, now with tears.

I could hardly speak, but I had to say it, "Man, that's what I call service: the best cream puff in the world, delivered right to my door!"

Our eyes followed Andy's as he turned his head and looked at the vanilla cream pastry still sitting on the pedestal of his hand. The top was missing. And most of the cream was between his fingers or soaking his shirt cuff. It was enough to send us into an extra round of hilarity. Though we had a near miss with the accident, I was afraid one of us might throw an aneurism with all the laughing.

I fell back into the rear seat of the car and nearly rolled to the floor of the taxi. That's when—through my tears—I saw the frog making his way from the bush. Unnoticed by the others who were still holding their sides, whooping and hollering, the frog hopped up to the seat through TaxiZack's open door and crawled toward his gym bag, which had been thrown to the floorboards from the seat in all the commotion. Then for one brief second the frog paused, turned to me, and winked.

Sure enough, it was BP. He smiled that satisfying, reassuring smile. Then with a single hop, he was in TaxiZack's gym bag, which I presumed would be his new home for the next week or so.

Everything settled down just as we heard the approaching sirens of the police and EMT unit that had been so quickly called to the scene by the firemen in their truck. Twenty minutes later, the cab company had delivered a new cab, and we were ready to be back on our way. It was dark, and by then Andy was closing up the sausage truck for the night. He invited us all to stop by to finish off his leftovers from the day, free of charge. The firemen, police, EMT, TaxiZack, and even the guy from the apartment were there, all celebrating the moment that had turned out so well, in spite of our near miss.

Before the evening was over, I'd given Andy the thumbs up for our LifeBet conversation, we'd chosen the book we would read together, our meeting time, and put it to the calendar. We would meet Monday nights, during that same time each week, after helping Andy shut down the truck.

Once I settled that, we said our good-byes. The cab company had already sent us a replacement cab. I slid into the backseat as TaxiZack climbed behind the wheel. A minute later, we were headed back home, passing through the very same intersection that earlier had been the scene of our little accident. Thoughts of that big red blur replayed in my mind.

No doubt, TaxiZack was thinking about the same thing. "That was a close one!" he said, and I think he shivered when he said it.

The light of a streetlamp flashed through the cab as we passed it. For a brief second, a small paper card shined in it and caught my attention. It was BP's calling card.

It was one last happy note from the frog, an indication that our story together didn't need to end. In fact, I would soon learn that it was just beginning.

We spoke eye-to-eye and made a new friend,
So saying goodbye doesn't mean it should end;
Just surf the Net, type the right key,
If you're willing to bet, you'll find me!
www.AmphibianDiaries.com

— WHAT NEXT? —

If you found this book as meaningful as I have, please consider buying a copy for a friend. Then be a LIFE*Bet* Maker, extend the invite to your friend, and enjoy sharing another round of the most critical conversation in life with your own LIFE*Bet* Taker.

PASS IT ON

Truth-Seeking in Summary

S

The **S**oul with a Hole
We are all seeking, satisfying life.

E

The **E**xpectation of Good
We will be satisfied by the Good Life only.

A

The **A**nswers from Outside the Box
We trust that we will be satisfied by our answers.

R

The **R**eason We Trust
We're wise to trust reasonable, right, and relevant things.

C

The **C**orresponding Perception
We're wise when our ideas and reality agree.

H

The **H**umble Heart
We learn wisdom from others, with others.

SEARCH

Wisdom Seeks Truth

Behold, thou desire truth in the inward parts:
and in the hidden part thou shalt make me
to know wisdom.

Acknowledgments

Frogs, like humans, are not wise when they are tadpoles. Wisdom is learned from others who have gone before. So frogs sit on, and leap from the shoulders of others. And humble and grateful frogs must identify and commend their instructors. This is why BP was very careful to express his gratitude for...

Dallas Theological Seminary, where the finest communicators, like Howard Hendricks, teach tadpoles to think as frogs.

Norman Geisler, the frog's teacher and primary source for communicating reasonable faith.

Nancy Zimpher, the primary catalyst to the frog's understanding of learning as a shared and developmental process.

James Hikins, who helped the frog communicate the connection between perception and reality.

Larry Moody and Bill Kraftson, cherished mentors to the frog, who along with their Search colleagues are remembered as the finest and most effective ministry.

Walt Hendricksen, the wisest of all the frog's teachers.

Young Life, the Sandlot small group: Cam Stewart, James King, Chris Welter, Alex Vichinski, Joey Meinerding, Josh Martin, Corey Hiegel, Kevin Peddicord, Zack Anderson, Andrew & Colin Berrigan, Dennis Cooper, and Matt Johnson. They happily hop with the frog at all times, even when the pond gets murky.

The many supporters, whose friendship with the frog is even more valuable than their financial support for publishing this book.

About the Author

A speaker, teacher, and mentor of spiritual development—John is not generally known for talking to frogs. But, BP Frog commissioned him to pass along the *Principles of Truth-Seeking* to empower the SEARCH.

He attended The Ohio State University on an athletic scholarship and graduated with a degree in Communication, then added a Master's of Biblical Studies at Dallas Theological Seminary, and did his doctoral studies in Educational Leadership Development at The Ohio State University.

John has worked for The Fellowship of Christian Athletes, served as a Senior Pastor, as Area Director for Search Ministries, and most recently as Director of The Heart for Home—a service dedicated to inviting friends into The Conversation of Life and God leading to Life in God's Love. He has lived by the code of *Amphibian Diaries* with countless stories of life change along the way. They are the tales that form the foundation for the book.

John and his wife, Susie, were teenage sweethearts, married young, and have spent forty years together in love in Columbus, Ohio. They have two daughters, and—so far—two grandchildren. John loves writing and telling stories with a creative and comedic flare. His hobbies often serve as subject matter for stories—their Golden Retriever therapy dogs and anything fast and daring, from speedboats and wave-runners to rappelling and sky-diving.

You may contact John directly via email:
BPFrog@AmphibianDiaries.com

CPSIA information can be obtained
at www.ICGtesting.com
Printed in the USA
LVHW081228201118
597764LV00006B/8/P